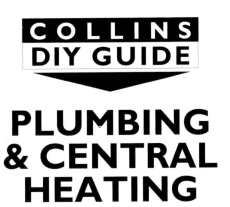

COLLINS
DIY GUIDE

PLUMBING & CENTRAL HEATING

COLLINS DIY GUIDE

PLUMBING & CENTRAL HEATING

JACKSON & DAY

HarperCollins*Publishers*

Published by HarperCollins Publishers
London

This book was created exclusively for
HarperCollins Publishers by
Jackson Day Jennings Ltd trading as
Inklink.

**Design, art direction
and project management**
Simon Jennings

Text
Albert Jackson
David Day

**Text and
editorial direction**
Albert Jackson

Illustrations editor
David Day

**Designer and
production assistant**
Alan Marshall

Illustrators
David Day
Robin Harris

Additional illustrations
Brian Craker
Michael Parr
Brian Sayers

First published in 1988
This edition published 1992,
reprinted in 1994

The text and illustrations in this book
were previously published in
Collins Complete DIY Manual

Copyright © 1986, 1988, 1992
HarperCollins Publishers

ISBN 0 00 412814 1

A CIP catalogue record for this book is
available from the British Library

Printed and bound in Hong Kong

Picture credits
Paul Chave: 51, 53, 69, 70, 71

CONTENTS

Cross-references
There are few DIY projects that do not require a combination of skills. Decorating a single room, for instance, might also involve modifying the plumbing or electrical wiring, installing ventilation or insulation, repairing the structure of the building and so on. As a result, you might have to refer to more than one section of this book. To help you locate the relevant sections, a symbol (▷) in the text refers you to a list of cross-references in the page margin. Those references printed in bold type are directly related to the task in hand. Other references which will broaden your understanding of the subject are printed in light-weight type.

PLUMBING – UNDERSTANDING THE SYSTEM

Over recent years, house owners and tenants have demonstrated a willingness, indeed a preference, to tackle their own plumbing repairs. As manufacturers responded to these demands by supplying hardware specially designed for them, householders in turn became even more ambitious, stimulating a growing industry aimed directly at the DIY market. Almost every aspect of home plumbing repair and improvement has been catered for with lightweight, attractive fittings which can be plumbed in quickly and confidently with traditional metal or modern plastic pipework. As usual, the need to save money has been the main incentive for the increased interest in DIY plumbing.

Materials alone are relatively expensive but the price of professional labour constitutes the greater part of any bill you incur, especially if it is necessary to call out a plumber at weekends or at an inconveniently late hour. Furthermore, stopping a leak quickly can save the expense and disappointment of ruined decorations or even the replacement of rotted household timbers. Even if you are insured against plumbing failures, it does not compensate for the disruption caused by major refurbishment. Lastly, there is the cost of water itself. A dripping tap wastes gallons of water a day, and if it's a hot water tap, there is the additional expense of heating it literally down the drain. The few pence spent on a washer can save you pounds.

Direct and indirect systems

You should familiarize yourself with the plumbing system in your own house so that you can isolate the relevant sections and drain the water during an emergency or prior to repairs and rerouting pipework.

Direct system
In many older properties, mains pressure is supplied to all cold water taps and WCs. Hot water is fed indirectly from the storage cistern via the hot water cylinder. The only advantage with this direct system is that drinking water can be drawn from any cold water tap in the house.

Indirect system
Most homes, and certainly modern houses, are plumbed with an indirect system. Water under mains pressure enters the house through a service pipe and proceeds via the rising main directly to the cold water storage cistern, normally situated in the roof space. A branch pipe from the rising main delivers drinking water to the kitchen sink, and possibly to a garden tap

through another pipe. All other cold water taps and appliances are fed indirectly, that is, under gravity pressure only, from the storage cistern. The hot water storage cylinder is also supplied with cold water from the same cistern. There it is heated either indirectly by the central heating system, or by electric immersion heaters, then drawn off from the top of the cylinder to hot water taps in the bathroom, kitchen and some of the bedrooms.

An indirect system provides several advantages to the householder and the water authority. Firstly, there is adequate water stored in the cistern to flush sanitary ware during a temporary mains failure. Also, as the major part of the supply is under relatively low pressure, an indirect system is reasonably quiet. (High mains pressure can cause 'water hammer' as the water tries to negotiate tight bends.) As few outlets are connected to the mains, there is less likelihood of impure water being siphoned back into the mains supply – an important consideration with regard to hygiene.

Drainage

Waste water is drained from either system in one of two ways. Up until the late 1940s or 50s, water was drained from baths, sinks and basins into a wastepipe which fed into a trapped gully at ground level. Toilet waste fed separately into a large diameter soil pipe running directly to the underground main drainage network.

A single stack waste system is used on later buildings where all waste drains into a single soil pipe. The only possible exception is the kitchen sink which still drains into a gully.

Rain water always feeds into a separate drain so that the house drainage system will not be flooded in the event of a storm (◁).

PLUMBING REGULATIONS

Your local water authority insists that certain regulations are observed whenever you alter existing installations or install new plumbing. The regulations are intended to preserve the health of the community and to reduce unnecessary waste. Except for straight-forward replacements, you should seek the advice of the appropriate authority on your local council. The methods described in this chapter comply with the regulations but a telephone call to the Town Hall will put you in touch with someone who can help you with queries about local requirements.

At the same time make sure that you do not contravene electrical regulations. All metal plumbing must be bonded to the Electricity Board's earth terminal near your meter. If you replace a section of metal plumbing with plastic, you may break the path to earth. Make sure that you reinstate the link (◁). If in doubt, consult a qualified electrician.

THE DIRECT SYSTEM

1. Water authority's stopcock

2. Service pipe

3. Main stopcock

4. Rising main
Supplies water to storage cylinder as well as cold water taps and WCs.

5. Cold water storage cistern

6. Hot water cylinder

7. Wastepipe
Surmounted by hopper head collects water from basin and bath.

8. Soil pipe
Separate pipe takes toilet waste to main drains.

9. Kitchen wastepipe
Kitchen sink drains into same gully as wastepipe from upstairs.

10. Trapped gully

Indirect system

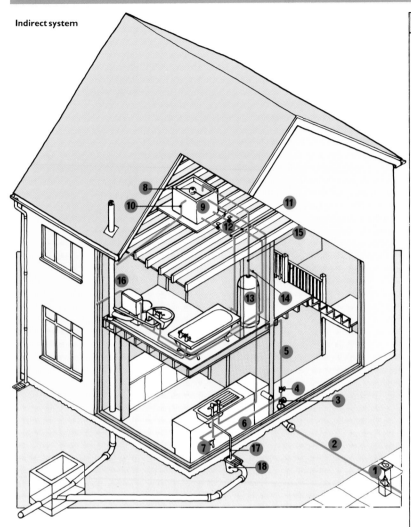

SEE ALSO

Details for: ▷
| Wet central heating | 49 |

THE INDIRECT SYSTEM

1 Water authority's stopcock
Water from the public main can be turned off at this stopcock. It works like a tap but also acts as a non-return valve so that, should mains pressure drop, water will not be siphoned from the household plumbing to contaminate the public supply.

2 Service pipe
From the stopcock onwards, the plumbing becomes the responsibility of the householder. The service pipe enters the house through a drainpipe packed with insulant to prevent water freezing.

3 Main stopcock
The water supply to the whole house is shut off at this point.

4 Draincock
A draincock here allows you to drain water from the rising main.

5 Rising main
Mains pressure water passes to the cold water cistern.

6 Drinking water
Drinking water is drawn off the rising main to the kitchen sink.

7 Garden tap
The water authority allows a garden tap to be supplied with mains pressure.

8 Float valve
Shuts off the supply from the rising main when the cistern is full.

9 Cold water storage cistern
Stores 230 to 360 litres (50 to 80 gallons) of water. Positioned in the roof, it provides sufficient 'head' or pressure to feed the whole house.

10 Overflow pipe
Also known as a warning pipe, it prevents an overflow by draining water to the outside of the house should the float valve fail to operate.

11 Cold feed pipes
Water is drawn off to the bathroom and to the hot water cylinder from the base of the storage cistern.

12 Cold feed valves
Valves at these points allow you to drain the cold water in the feed pipe without having to drain the whole cistern as well. Alternatively, they may be placed in the airing cupboard.

13 Hot water cylinder
There may be a draincock in this position to empty the cylinder.

14 Hot feed pipe
All hot water is fed from this point.

15 Vent pipe
A vent pipe drains into the cistern to allow for expansion of heated water and to vent air from the system.

16 Single stack soil pipe

17 Sink waste
Drains into trapped gully.

18 Trapped gully

Direct system

• **Central heating**
Omitted for clarity. (▷)

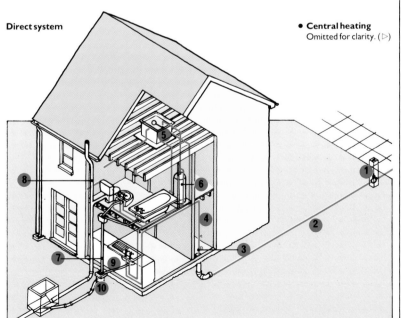

DRAINING THE SYSTEM

You will have to drain at least part of any plumbing system before you can work on it, and if you detect a leak, you will have to drain the relevant section quickly, so find out where the valves, stopcock and drain cocks are situated before you are faced with an emergency.

Draining cold water taps and pipes

● Turn off the main stopcock on the rising main to cut off the supply to the kitchen tap. (And every other cold tap on a direct system.)
● Open the tap until the water ceases to flow.
● To isolate bathroom taps, close the valve on the appropriate cold feed pipe from the storage cistern and open all taps on that section. If you can't find a valve, rest a wooden batten across the cistern and tie the arm of the float valve to it. This will shut off the supply to the cistern so you can empty it by running all the cold taps in the bathroom. If you can't get into the loft, turn off the main stopcock, then run the cold taps.

Draining hot water taps and pipes

● Turn off immersion heaters or boiler.
● Close the valve on the cold feed pipe to the cylinder and run the hot taps. Even when the water stops flowing, the cylinder will still be full.
● If there is no valve on the cold feed pipe, tie up the float valve arm, then turn on bathroom cold taps to empty the storage cistern. (If you run the hot taps first, the water stored in the cistern will flush out all your hot water from the cylinder.) When cold taps run dry, open the hot taps. In an emergency, run the hot and cold taps together to clear the pipes as quickly as possible. (With a direct system you have no choice but to drain the system via the hot taps.)

Draining a WC cistern

● To merely empty the cistern itself, tie up the float valve arm (See above) and flush the WC.
● To empty the pipe supplying the cistern, either turn off the main stopcock on a direct system, or, on an indirect system, close the valve on the cold feed from the storage cistern. Alternatively, tie up the float valve arm and empty the storage cistern through the cold taps. Flush the WC until no more water enters its cistern.

Draining the cold water storage cistern

● To drain the storage cistern in the roof, close the main stopcock on the rising main then open all the cold taps in the bathroom. (Hot taps on a direct system.) Bail out the residue of water at the bottom of the cistern.

Draining the hot water cylinder

If the cylinder springs a leak, or you intend to replace it, first turn off immersion heaters or boiler, then shut off its cold water supply or drain the cold water cistern (See above). Run hot water from taps.
● If the water is heated by immersion heaters only, there should be a draincock on the cold feed pipe just before it enters the cylinder. Attach a hose to it and drain the water still in the cylinder into the nearest drain or sink at a lower level.
● If the water is heated by a boiler which is not part of a central heating system, empty the cylinder with a hose from the draincock on the return pipe next to the boiler.
● When a boiler heats the water and the central heating system, empty the cylinder from the draincock on its cold feed pipe from the storage cistern. (The primary circuit, which heats the radiators and the heat exchanger in the cylinder (◁), is still filled with water. That circuit is drained when necessary from the draincock next to the boiler. Close both valves on radiators (◁) if you do not need to empty them.)
● If no draincocks are provided, disconnect the vent pipe (◁) and siphon the cylinder with a hosepipe.

Closing a float valve
Cut off the supply of water to a storage cistern by tying the float arm to a batten.

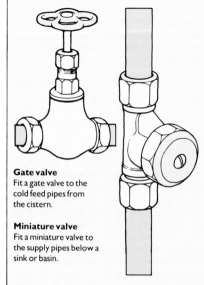

ADDING EXTRA VALVES

You will have to drain off a substantial part of a typical plumbing installation even for a simple washer replacement unless you divide the system into relatively short pipe runs with valves.
● Install a gate valve on both cold feed pipes running from the cold water storage cistern. This will save you having to drain gallons of water in order to isolate pipes and appliances on the low-pressure cold and hot-water supply.
● When you are fitting new taps, take the opportunity to fit miniature valves on the supply pipes just below the sink or basin. In future, you will be able to isolate an individual tap in moments when you have to repair it.

Gate valve
Fit a gate valve to the cold feed pipes from the cistern.

Miniature valve
Fit a miniature valve to the supply pipes below a sink or basin.

DRAINING AND REFILLING THE WHOLE SYSTEM

Drain the complete plumbing system when you intend to leave the house unoccupied for a long period during the winter, otherwise you run the risk of a 'freeze up' which may burst pipes or force joints apart. Drain the system in the following order.
● Switch off the boiler or immersion heaters. Rake out a solid fuel boiler and allow it to cool.
● Turn off the main stopcock on the rising main, and run off the water from all cold and hot taps.
● If there is a draincock on the rising main, drain what water is left in the pipe from that point.
● Flush the WCs.
● Drain the hot water cylinder.
● Don't bother to drain the water from the central heating system but make sure it contains antifreeze (▷).
● Place a note prominently to remind yourself to fill the system before lighting the boiler or switching on the immersion heater.
● If you can expect very low temperatures where you live, pour some salt into the WC pan to stop the water freezing in the trap. Treat other traps similarly.

Refilling the system
To refill the system, close all taps and draincocks, then open the main stopcock. As the system fills, check that float valves are operating smoothly. Air trapped in the system may cause taps to splutter for a while. If it doesn't clear naturally, flush it out with mains pressure (See below).

CURING AN AIR LOCK

Air trapped in the system can cause a tap to splutter or fail completely. Force the air out using mains water pressure.

Attach a length of hosepipe between the affected tap and the cold water tap over the kitchen sink. (Any cold water tap on a direct system.) Leave both taps open for a short while and try the air-locked tap again. If necessary, repeat the procedure until water runs freely.

If you have to use a long hose, it will contain a lot of water so drain it into the kitchen sink before you move it.

EMERGENCY REPAIRS

Every householder should master the simple techniques for coping with emergency repairs in order to avoid unnecessary damage to property, and the high cost of calling out a plumber at short notice. All you need is a simple tool kit and a few spare parts.

Thawing frozen pipes

Insulate your pipework and fittings, particularly those in the loft or under the floor (▷), to stop them freezing. If you leave the house unheated for a long time during the winter, drain the system (See left). Cure dripping taps so that leaking water does not freeze in your drainage system overnight.

If water will not flow from a tap or a cistern refuses to fill in cold weather, a plug of ice may have formed in one of the supply pipes. The plug cannot be in a pipe supplying those taps or float valves which are working normally, so you should be able to trace the blockage fairly quickly. In fact, freezing usually occurs first in the roof space.

As copper pipework transmits heat readily, use a hairdryer to warm the suspect pipe, starting as close as possible to the tap or valve, then work along it. Leave the tap open so that water can flow normally as soon as the ice thaws. If you cannot heat the pipe with a hairdryer, wrap it in a hot towel or hang a rubber hot water bottle over it.

Dealing with a nailed pipe

Unless you are absolutely sure where your pipes run, it is all too easy to nail through one of them when fixing a loose floorboard. You may be able to detect a hissing sound as water escapes under pressure, but more than likely you won't notice your mistake until a wet patch appears on the ceiling below or some problem associated with damp occurs at a later date. With the nail in place, water will leak relatively slowly so don't pull it out until you have drained the pipework and can repair the leak. If you pull it out by lifting a floorboard, put it back immediately.

If you plan to lay fitted carpet, you can paint pipe runs on the floorboards to avoid a similar accident.

Patching a leak

During freezing conditions, water within a pipe will turn to ice which expands until it eventually splits the walls of the tube or forces a joint apart. Copper pipework is more likely to split than lead which can stretch to accommodate the expansion, taking a few hard winters before reaching breaking point. Patch either pipe as described right but close up a split in lead beforehand using gentle taps with a hammer. Repairing lead permanently is not easy, so hire a plumber as soon as you have contained the leak.

The only other reason for leaking plumbing is mechanical failure, either through deterioration or because the plumber failed to make a completely waterproof joint.

If you can, make a permanent repair by inserting a new section of pipe or replace a leaking joint. If it is a compression joint that has failed, try tightening it first (▷). However, you may have to make an emergency repair for the time being. Always drain the pipe first unless it is frozen, in which case make the repair before it thaws.

Using a hose and Jubilee clips
Cut a length of garden hose to cover the leak, and slit it lengthwise so that you can slip it over the pipe. Bind the hose with two or three Jubilee clips. (Normally used to attach hoses on a car engine.) If you cannot obtain clips, twist wire loops around the hose with pliers.

Patching with epoxy putty
The putty is supplied in two parts which begin to harden as soon as they are mixed, giving you about 20 minutes to complete the repair. The putty will adhere to most metals and hard plastic. Although it is better to insert a new length of pipe, epoxy putty will produce a fairly long-term repair.

Use abrasive paper or wire wool to clean a 25 to 50mm (1 to 2in) length of pipe on each side of the leak. Mix the putty thoroughly and press it into the hole or around a joint, building it to a thickness of 3 to 6mm (⅛ to ¼in). It will cure to full strength within 24 hours, but you can run low pressure water immediately if you bind the putty with self-adhesive tape.

SEE ALSO

Details for:	▷
Insulating pipes	65
Compression joints	22
Antifreeze/inhibitor	55
Jointing pipes	20-27

Thawing a frozen pipe
Play a hairdryer along a frozen pipe working away from the blocked tap or valve.

Binding a split pipe
Bind a length of hosepipe around a split pipe with hose clips.

Smoothing epoxy putty
When you have patched a hole with epoxy putty, smooth it with a damp, soapy cloth for a neat finish.

9

REPAIRING A LEAKING TAP

A tap may leak for a number of reasons but none of them are difficult to deal with. When water drips from a spout, for instance, it is most likely caused by a faulty washer, or if the tap is old, the seat against which the washer is compressed may be worn also. If water leaks from beneath the head of the tap when it's in use, the gland packing or 'O' ring needs replacing.

When working on taps, insert the plug and lay a towel in the bottom of the sink or bath to catch small objects.

SEE ALSO

◁ Details for:
Spanners and wrenches   75-76

Traditional pillar tap
The components of a pillar tap
1 Capstan head
2 Metal shroud
3 Gland nut
4 Spindle
5 Headgear nut
6 Jumper
7 Washer
8 Tap body
9 Seat
10 Tail

Bib tap

Pillar tap

Reverse pressure tap

Shrouded-head tap

REMOVING A SHROUDED HEAD

On most modern taps the head and cover is in one piece. You will have to remove it to expose the headgear nut. Often a retaining screw is hidden beneath the coloured hot/cold disc in the centre of the head. Prise it out with the point of a knife. If there is no retaining screw, the head will pull off, or remove it by continuing to unscrew the head as if you were turning the tap on in the normal way.

Replacing a washer

To replace the washer in a traditional bib or pillar tap, first drain the supply pipe, then open the valve as far as possible before dismantling either of the taps.

If the tap is shrouded with a metal cover, unscrew it, by hand if possible, or tape the jaws of a wrench to protect the chrome finish.

Lift up the cover to reveal the headgear nut just above the body of the tap. Slip a narrow spanner onto the nut and unscrew it (**1**) until you can lift out the entire headgear assembly.

The jumper, to which the washer is fixed, fits into the bottom of the headgear. With some taps, the jumper is removed along with the headgear (**2**) but in other cases it will be lying inside the tap body.

The washer itself may be pressed over a small button in the centre of the jumper (**3**), in which case, prise it off with a screwdriver. If the washer is held in place by a nut, it can be difficult to remove. Allow penetrating oil to soften any corrosion, then, holding the jumper stem with pliers, unscrew the nut with a snug-fitting spanner (**4**). (If the nut will not budge, replace the whole jumper and washer.) Fit a new washer and retaining nut, then reassemble the tap.

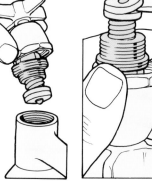
1 Loosen headgear nut

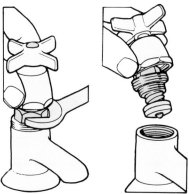
2 Lift out headgear

3 Prise off washer

4 Or undo fixing nut

Replacing a washer in a reverse-pressure tap

The distinctive reverse-pressure tap is like an upside down version of a conventional tap – the washer is screwed upwards against the seat. When replacing a washer, there is no need to shut off the water because an integral check valve closes automatically as the body is removed.

Loosen the retaining nut above the tap body (**1**), then unscrew the body itself as if you were opening the tap. Water will run until the check valve operates, but continue to unscrew the body (**2**) until it drops into your hand.

Tap the nozzle on the floor (**3**), not on a ceramic basin, then turn the body upside down to tip out the finned, anti-splash device. Prise the combined jumper and washer from the end of the anti-splash device (**4**) and replace it.

Reassemble the tap in the reverse order, remembering that the body is screwed back clockwise when viewed from above.

1 Loosen retaining nut

2 Remove tap body

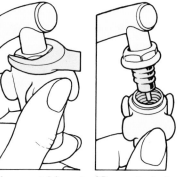
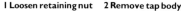
3 Tap nozzle on floor

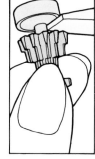
4 Prise off jumper

REPLACING 'O' RINGS ON MIXER TAPS

Each valve on a mixer tap is fitted with a washer like a conventional tap but in most mixers, the gland packing has been replaced by a rubber 'O' ring.

Having removed the shrouded head, take out the circlip holding the spindle in place (1). Remove the spindle, and slip the old 'O' ring out of its groove (2). Replace it with a new one and reassemble the tap.

 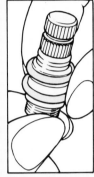

1 Remove circlip   2 Roll ring from groove

The base of a mixer's swivel spout is sealed with a washer or 'O' ring. If water seeps from that junction, turn off both valves and unscrew the spout, or remove the retaining screw (3) on one side. Note the type of seal and buy a matching replacement.

3 Remove screw to release mixer spout

MAINTAINING STOPCOCKS AND VALVES

Stopcocks and gate valves are used rarely so their maintenance is often neglected, but, if they fail to work just when you need them, you could have a serious problem on your hands.

Make sure they are operating smoothly by closing and opening them from time to time. If the spindles move stiffly, lubricate them with a little penetrating oil. Unlike a gate valve, a stopcock is fitted with a standard washer but as it is hardly ever under pressure, it is unlikely to wear. However, the gland packing on both the gate valve and stopcock may need attention (See right).

REPAIRING SEATS AND GLANDS

Regrinding the seat

If a tap continues to drip after you have replaced the washer, the seat is probably worn and water is leaking past the washer.

One way to cure it is to grind the seat flat with a specialized reseating tool rented from a hire company. Remove the headgear and jumper so that you can screw the tool into the body of the tap.

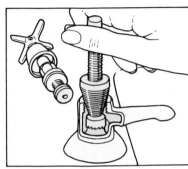

1 Revolve the tool to smooth the seat

Adjust the cutter until it is in contact with the seat then turn the handle to smooth the seat (1). Alternatively, cover the old seat with a nylon substitute, sold with a matching jumper and washer (2). Drop the seating component over the old seat, replace the jumper and assemble the tap. Close the tap to force the seat in position.

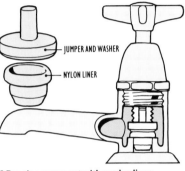

2 Repair a worn seat with a nylon liner

Curing a leaking gland

The head of a tap is fixed to a shaft or spindle which is screwed up or down to control the flow of water. The spindle passes through a gland, also known as a stuffing box, on top of the headgear assembly (▷). A watertight packing is forced into the gland by a nut to prevent water leaking past the spindle when the tap is turned on. If water drips from under the head of the tap, the gland packing has failed and should be replaced.

Some taps incorporate a rubber 'O' ring which slips over the spindle to perform the same function as the packing (See left).

Replacing the gland packing
There is no need to turn off the supply of water to replace gland packing; just make sure the tap is turned off fully.

To remove a cross or capstan head,

expose a fixing screw by picking out the plastic plug in the centre of the head, or look for a screw holding it at the side. Lift off the head by rocking it from side to side, or tap it gently from below with a hammer.

If the head is stuck firmly, open the tap as far as possible, unscrew the cover and wedge wooden packing between it and the headgear (1). Closing the tap jacks the head off the spindle.

Lift off the head and cover, then attempt to seal the leak by tightening the gland nut. If that fails, remove the nut and pick out the old packing with a small screwdriver.

To replace the packing, use special impregnated twine from a plumbers' merchant or twist a thread from PTFE (polytetrafluorethylene) tape (▷). Wind it around the spindle and pack it into the gland with a screwdriver (2).

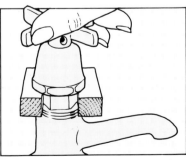

1 Jack the head off a tap with wooden packing

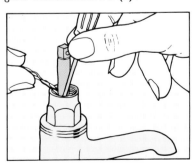

2 Stuff a thread of PTFE tape into the gland

GLAND PACKING

Gland packing
Older style taps are sealed with a watertight packing around the spindle.

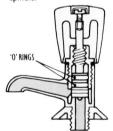

'O' RINGS

'O' ring seal
More modern taps are sealed with rubber rings in place of the gland packing.

MAINTAINING WC AND STORAGE CISTERNS

There is no reason why anyone should have to call out a plumber to service a WC cistern. Most of them are situated directly behind the WC pan so they are readily accessible, but even an old-fashioned, high-level cistern can be reached from a stepladder. The design of a cistern mechanism varies so little that components are available from the stock of any plumbers' merchant and many DIY outlets.

The water storage cistern in the loft is simply a container. Apart from a leak, which is unlikely to occur with a modern cistern, the only problems to arise are as a result of float valve failure. The float valve in a storage cistern is basically the same as that used for the WC cistern.

Direct action cistern
The components of a typical direct action WC cistern.
1 Overflow
2 Float
3 Float arm
4 Float valve
5 Siphon
6 Wire link
7 Flushing lever
8 Flap valve
9 Perforated plate
10 Sealing washer
11 Retaining nut
12 Flush pipe connector

DIRECT ACTION WC CISTERN

Most modern WCs are washed down with direct flushing cisterns. Water enters an empty cistern through a valve which is opened and closed by the action of a hollow float attached to one end of a rigid arm. As the water rises in the cistern, it lifts the float until the other end of the arm eventually closes the valve and shuts off the supply.

Flushing is carried out by depressing a lever which lifts a perforated metal plate at the bottom of an inverted 'U' bend tube (siphon). As the plate rises, the perforations are sealed by a flexible plastic diaphragm (flap valve) so that the plate can displace a body of water over the 'U' bend to promote a siphoning action. The resulting water pressure behind the diaphragm lifts it again so that the contents of the cistern flow up through the perforations in the plate, over the 'U' bend, and down the flush pipe. As the water level in the cistern drops, so does the float, opening the float valve to refill the cistern.

There are few problems associated with this type of cistern and all of them can be solved with regular maintenance. A faulty float valve or poorly adjusted arm allows water to leak into the cistern until it drips from the overflow pipe running to the outside of the house. Slow or noisy filling is often rectified by replacing the float valve. If the cistern will not flush until the lever is operated several times, the flap valve is probably worn and needs replacing.

Tying up a float arm
Tie the arm to a batten placed across the cistern when you need to shut off the supply of water.

Replacing the flap valve

If the WC cistern will not flush first time, take off the lid and check that the lever is actually operating the mechanism. If it is working normally, replace the flap valve in the siphon. Shut off the water by tying up the float valve arm (◁), and flush the cistern.

Use a large wrench to unscrew the nut holding the flush pipe to the underside of the cistern (1). Move the pipe to one side.

Release the remaining nut which clamps the siphon to the base of the cistern (2). A little water will run out as you loosen the nut so have a bucket handy. (It's just possible that the siphon is bolted to the base of the cistern instead of being clamped by one large retaining nut.)

Disconnect the flushing arm and ease the siphon out of the cistern. Lift the diaphragm off the metal plate (3) and substitute one of the same size. Reassemble the flushing mechanism in the reverse order and attach the flush pipe to the cistern.

1 Release flush pipe   2 Loosen retaining nut   3 Lift off flap valve

Making a new link

If the flushing lever feels slack and the cistern will not even attempt to flush, look to see if the wire link at the end of the flushing arm is intact.

Retrieve the broken pieces from the cistern and bend a new link from a piece of thick wire. If you have thin wire only, twist the ends together with pliers to make a temporary repair until you can buy a new link.

Curing continuous running water

If you notice water continuously trickling into the pan from the flush pipe, lift out the siphon as described above and renew the washer which seals the siphon to the base of the cistern. Make sure the replacement is identical.

DIAPHRAGM VALVES

The pivoting end of the float arm on a diaphragm valve presses against the end of a small plastic piston which moves the large rubber diaphragm to seal the water outlet.

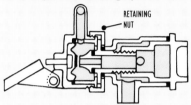

1 Diaphragm valve: retaining cap to the front

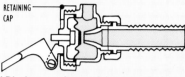

2 Diaphragm valve: retaining nut to the rear

Replacing the diaphragm

Turn off the water supply then unscrew the large retaining cap. Depending on the model, the nut may be screwed onto the end of the valve (1) or it may be behind it (2).

With the latter type of valve, slide out the cartridge inside the body (3) to find the diaphragm behind it. With the former, you will find a similar piston and diaphragm immediately behind the retaining cap (4).

Wash out the valve before assembling it along with the new diaphragm.

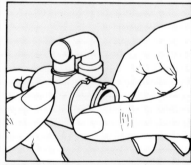

3 Slide out piston to release the diaphragm

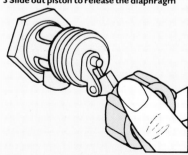

4 Remove cap and pull float arm to find valve

RENOVATING FLOAT VALVES

A faulty float valve is responsible for most of the difficulties that arise with WC and water storage cisterns. Traditionally, the water outlet in the valve is sealed with a washer, but later patterns of valve utilize a large diaphragm instead, designed to protect the mechanism from scale deposits. Both types of valve are still widely available. If the outlet isn't sealed properly, water continues to feed into the cistern until it escapes to the outside via the overflow pipe. You may be able to solve the problem by simply adjusting the float arm, but more than likely, the washer or diaphragm is worn.

Portsmouth pattern valves

In a Portsmouth pattern valve, a piston moves horizontally inside the hollow metal body. The float arm, pivoting on a split pin, moves the piston back and forth to control the flow of water. A washer trapped in the end of the piston finally seals the outlet by pressing against the valve seat.

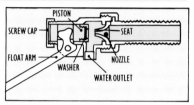

Portsmouth pattern valve

Replacing a washer

If you have to force the valve closed to stop water dripping, replace the washer. Cut off the supply of water to the cistern (▷), and although it is not essential, flush the cistern in case you drop a component into the water. Remove the split pin from beneath the valve and detach the float arm.

If there is a screw cap on the end of the valve body, remove it (1). You may have to apply a little penetrating oil to ease the threads, and grip the cap with slip joint pliers (▷).

Insert the tip of a screwdriver in the slot beneath the valve body and slide the piston out (2).

To remove the captive washer, unscrew the end cap of the piston with pliers. Steady the piston by holding a screwdriver in its slot (3).

Pick the old washer out of the cap (4) but before replacing it, clean the piston with fine wire wool. Some pistons do not have a removable end cap, and the washer must be dug out with a pointed knife. Take care when replacing this type of washer which is a tight fit within a groove in the piston.

Use wet and dry paper wrapped around a dowel rod to clean inside the valve body but take care not to damage the valve seat at the far end.

Reassemble the piston and smear it with a light coating of petroleum jelly. Rebuild the valve and connect the float arm. Restore the supply of water and adjust the arm to regulate the water level in the cistern (▷).

Croydon pattern valve
Only old fashioned cisterns will be fitted with this valve. The piston travels vertically to close against the seat. Replace the washer as described left.

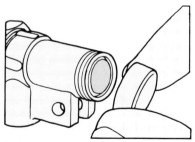

1 Take screw cap from the end of the valve

2 Slide the piston out with a screwdriver

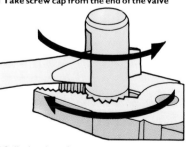

3 Split the piston into two parts

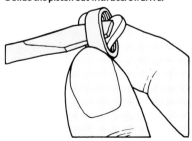

4 Pick out the washer with a screwdriver

RENOVATING VALVES AND FLOATS

Adjusting the float arm

Adjust the float to maintain the optimum level of water which is about 25mm (1in) below the outlet of the overflow pipe.

The arm on a Portsmouth valve is a solid metal rod. Bend it downward slightly to reduce the water level or straighten it to admit more water (**1**).

The arm on a diaphragm valve is fitted with an adjusting screw which presses on the end of the piston. Release the lock nut and turn the screw towards the valve to lower the water level or away from it to allow the water to rise (**2**).

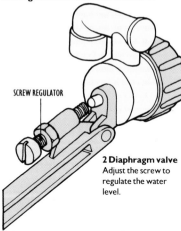

1 Straighten or bend a metal float arm

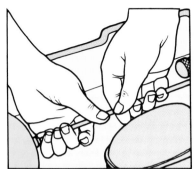

SCREW REGULATOR

2 Diaphragm valve
Adjust the screw to regulate the water level.

Replacing the float

Modern plastic floats rarely leak but old style metal floats do corrode eventually, allowing water to seep into the ball. It gradually sinks until it won't ride high enough to close the valve.

Unscrew the float and shake it to test whether there is water inside. If you can't replace it for several days, lay the ball on a bench and enlarge the leaking hole with a screwdriver, then pour out the water. Replace the float and cover it with a plastic bag, tying the neck tightly around the float arm.

Curing noisy cisterns

Cisterns that fill noisily can be a real source of annoyance, particularly if the WC is situated right next to a bedroom. It was once permitted to screw a pipe into the outlet of a valve so that it hung vertically below the level of the water. It solved the problem of water splashing into the cistern but water authorities were alarmed at the possibility of water 'back-siphoning' through the silencer tube into the mains supply. Although rigid tubes are banned nowadays, you are permitted to fit a valve with a flexible plastic silencer tube because it will seal itself by collapsing should back-siphonage occur.

A silencer tube can also prevent water hammer – a rythmic thudding that reverberates along the pipework. It is largely the result of ripples on the surface of the water in a cistern, caused by a heavy flow from the float valve. As the water rises, the float arm, bouncing on the ripples, hammers the valve and the sound is amplified and transmitted along the pipes. A flexible plastic silencer tube will eliminate ripples by introducing water below the surface.

If the water pressure through the valve is too high, the arm oscillates as it tries to close the valve – another cause of water hammer. Cure it by fitting an equilibrium valve. As water flows through the valve, some of it is introduced behind the piston or diaphragm to equalize the pressure on each side so that the valve closes smoothly and silently.

Before swapping your present valve, check that the pipework is clipped securely (◁) to cut down vibration.

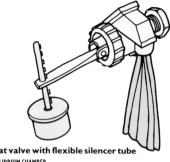

Float valve with flexible silencer tube

EQUILIBRIUM CHAMBER

CAP
WASHER

WASHER

FLOAT ARM

HOLLOW PISTON   WATER OUTLET

Equilibrium valve

Changing a float valve

Turn off the supply of water to the cistern and flush the pipework, then use a spanner to loosen the tap connector joining the supply pipe to the float valve stem. Remove the float arm, then unscrew the fixing nut on the outside of the cistern and pull out the valve.

Fit the new valve and, if possible, use the same tap connector to join it to the supply pipe. Adjust and tighten the fixing nuts to clamp the new valve to the cistern, then turn on the water and adjust the float arm.

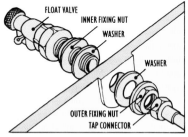

FLOAT VALVE

INNER FIXING NUT

WASHER

WASHER

OUTER FIXING NUT
TAP CONNECTOR

Replacing a float valve
Clamp a valve to the cistern with fixing nuts.

CHOOSING THE RIGHT PRESSURE

Float valves are made to suit different water pressures: low, medium and high (LP, MP, HP). It is important to choose a valve of the correct pressure or it may take a long time to fill. Conversely, the water pressure may be so high that the valve leaks continuously. Those fed direct from the mains should be HP valves, whereas most domestic WC cisterns require an LP valve. If the head (the height of the cistern above the float valve) is greater than 13.5m (45ft), fit an MP valve. In rare cases where the head exceeds 30m (100ft), fit an HP valve. In an apartment using a packaged plumbing system (a storage cistern built on top of the hot water cylinder (◁), the pressure may be so low that you will have to fit a 'full way' valve to the WC cistern to get it to fill quickly. If you live in an area where water pressure fluctuates a great deal, fit an equilibrium valve (See left).

To alter the pressure, replace the nozzle inside a modern Portsmouth or diaphragm valve. If the valve is a very old pattern, you will have to swap it for another one of a different pressure.

MAINTAINING A DRAINAGE SYSTEM

A drainage system is designed to carry dirty water and WC waste from the various appliances to underground drains leading to the main sewer. The different branches of the waste system are protected by 'U' bend traps full of water to stop drain smells fouling the house. Depending on the age of your house, it will have a two-pipe system or a single stack. Because the two-pipe system has been in use for very much longer, it is still the more common of the two. Use similar methods to maintain either system.

Two-pipe system

The wastepipes of older houses are divided into two separate systems. WC waste is fed into a large diameter, vertical soil pipe which leads directly to the underground drains. To discharge drain gases at a safe height, and to make sure that back-siphoning cannot empty the WC traps, the soil pipe is vented to the open air above the guttering.

Individual branch pipes, leading from upstairs wash basins and baths, drain into an open hopper which funnels the water into another vertical wastepipe. Instead of feeding directly into the underground drains, this wastepipe terminates over a yard gully – another trap covered by a grid. A separate wastepipe from the kitchen sink normally drains into the same gully.

The yard gully and soil pipe discharge into an underground inspection chamber, or manhole. These chambers provide access to the main drains for clearing blockages, and you will find one wherever the drain changes direction on its way to the sewer. At the last inspection chamber, just before the drain enters the sewer, there is an interceptor trap, the final barrier to drain gases, and in this case, sewer rats.

Single stack system

Since the 1960s, most houses have been drained using a single stack system. Waste from basins, baths and WCs is fed into the same vertical soil pipe or stack, which, unlike the two-pipe system, is often built inside the house. A single stack system must be designed carefully to prevent a heavy discharge of waste from one appliance siphoning the trap of another, and to avoid the possibility of WC waste blocking other branch pipes. The vent pipe of the stack terminates above the roof and is capped with an open cage to prevent birds sealing the pipe by nesting in it.

The kitchen sink can be drained through the same stack but it is still common practice to drain sink waste into a yard gully. Nowadays, wastepipes must pass through the grid, stopping short of the water in the gully trap so that even when the grid becomes blocked with leaves, the waste can discharge unobstructed into the gully. Alternatively, it will be a back-inlet gully with the waste pipe entering below ground level.

A downstairs WC is sometimes drained through its own branch drain to an inspection chamber.

RESPONSIBILITY FOR THE DRAINS

Where a house is drained individually, the whole system up to where it joins the sewer is the responsibility of the householder. Where a house is connected to a communal drainage system linking several houses, the arrangement for maintenance, including the clearance of blockages, is not so straightforward.

If the drains were constructed prior to 1937, the local council is responsible for cleansing but can reclaim the cost of repairing any part of the communal system from the householders. After that date, the entire responsibility falls upon the householders collectively, so that they are required to share the cost of both repair and cleansing of the drains up to the sewer, no matter where the problem occurs. Contact the Environmental Health Officer of your local council to find out who is responsible for your drains.

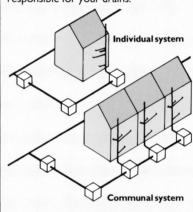

Individual system

Communal system

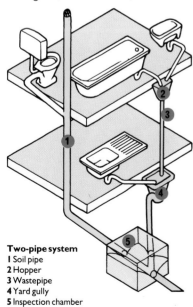

Two-pipe system
1 Soil pipe
2 Hopper
3 Wastepipe
4 Yard gully
5 Inspection chamber

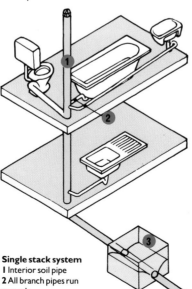

Single stack system
1 Interior soil pipe
2 All branch pipes run to stack
3 Inspection chamber

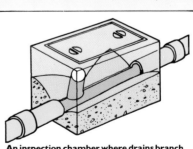

An inspection chamber where drains branch

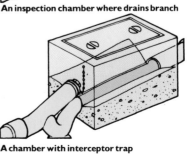

A chamber with interceptor trap

Pre-fabricated chamber
The inspection chambers of a modern drainage system may be cylindrical pre-fabricated units. There may not be an interceptor trap in the chamber before the sewer.

CLEARING A BLOCKED WASTE SYSTEM

Don't ignore the early signs of an imminent blockage of the wastepipe from a sink, bath or basin. If the water drains away slowly, use a chemical cleaner to remove a partial blockage before you are faced with clearing a serious obstruction. If a wastepipe blocks without warning, try a series of measures to locate and clear the obstruction.

Cleansing the wastepipe

Grease, hair and particles of kitchen debris build up gradually within the traps and wastepipes. Regular cleaning with a proprietary chemical drain cleaner will keep the waste system clear and sweet smelling.

If water drains sluggishly, use a cleaner immediately, following the manufacturer's instructions with particular regard to safety. Always wear protective gloves when handling chemical cleaners and keep them out of the reach of children.

If unpleasant odours linger after you have cleaned the waste, pour a little disinfectant into the basin overflow.

USING COMPRESSED AIR TO CLEAR A SINK

Clear a blocked waste with compressed air using a simple hand operated tool. Three strokes of the hand pump builds a low pressure which will clear most blockages without blowing apart push-fit joints. Place the rubber nozzle of the tool into the waste outlet and squeeze the trigger. If the blockage persists, increase the pressure gradually.

Using a compressed air gun
The tool is supplied with a range of soft adaptor nozzles to fit different sizes of sink plug. Press the nozzle into the waste and squeeze the trigger to clear a blockage.

Using a plunger

If a basin fails to empty while others are functioning normally, the blockage must be somewhere along its individual branch pipe. Before you attempt to locate the blockage, try forcing it out of the pipe with a sink plunger. Smear the rim of the rubber cap with petroleum jelly, then lower it into the blocked basin to cover the waste outlet. Make sure there is enough water in the basin to cover the cup. Hold a wet cloth in the overflow with one hand while you pump the handle of the plunger up and down a few times. The waste may not clear immediately if the blockage is merely forced further along the pipe, so repeat the process until the water drains away. If it will not clear after several attempts, try clearing the trap, or use compressed air to clear the pipe (See left).

Clearing the trap

The trap, situated immediately below the waste outlet of a sink or basin, is basically a bent tube designed to hold water to seal out drain odours. Traps become blocked when debris collects at the lowest point of the bend. Place a bucket under the basin to catch the water then use a wrench to release the cleaning eye at the base of a standard trap. Alternatively, remove the large access cap on a bottle trap by hand. If there is no provision for gaining access to the trap, unscrew the connecting nuts and remove the entire trap. (Take the opportunity to scrub it out with detergent before replacing it.)

Let the contents of the trap drain into the bucket, then bend a hook on the end of a length of wire to probe the section of wastepipe beyond the trap. If the pipe is clear but the blockage is still intact, it must be in the branch running to the soil stack or outside to the hopper and vertical wastepipe.

Cleaning the branch pipe

Quite often, a vertical pipe from the trap joins a virtually horizontal section of the wastepipe. There should be an access plug built into the joint so that you can clear the horizontal pipe. Have a bowl ready to collect any trapped water then unscrew the plug by hand. Use a length of hooked wire to probe the branch pipe. If you locate a blockage which seems very firm, rent a drain auger (◁) from a tool hire company to clear the pipework.

If there is no access plug, remove the trap and probe the pipe with an auger. If the wastepipe is constructed with push-fit joints, you can dismantle it.

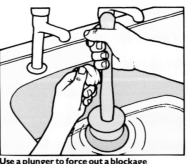
Use a plunger to force out a blockage

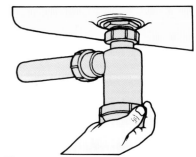
Unscrew the access cap on a bottle trap

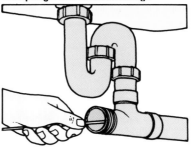
Use hooked wire to probe a branch pipe

Tubular trap
If the access cap to the cleaning eye is stiff, remove it with a wrench.

Bottle trap
A bottle trap can be cleared easily because the whole base unscrews by hand.

CLEARING A STACK OR GULLY

If several fittings are draining poorly the vertical stack itself is probably obstructed. The hopper and downpipe as well as the yard gully are frequently blocked with leaves in the autumn. It may not be obvious when you empty a hand basin, but the contents of a bath will almost certainly cause the hopper or gully to overflow. Clear the blockage urgently to avoid penetrating damp (▷).

Cleaning out the hopper and drainpipe

Wearing protective gloves, scoop out the debris from the hopper then gently probe the drainpipe with a cane to check that it is free. Clear the bottom end of the pipe with a piece of bent wire. If an old cast iron wastepipe has been replaced with a modern plastic type, you may find cleaning eyes or access plugs at strategic points for clearing a blockage.

While you are on the ladder, scrub the inside of the hopper and disinfect it to prevent stale odours entering a nearby bathroom.

Unblocking a yard gully

Unless you decide to hire an auger, there is little option but to clear a blocked gully by hand, but by the time it overflows, the water in the gully will be quite deep so try bailing some of it out with a small disposable container. Wearing rubber gloves, scoop out the debris from the trap until the remaining water disperses.

Rinse the gully with a hose and cleanse it with disinfectant. Scrub the grid as clean as possible or alternatively, burn off accumulated grime from a metal grid with a gas torch (▷).

If a flooded gully appears to be clear, and yet the water will not drain away, try to locate the blockage at the nearest inspection chamber (▷).

Bail out the water then clear a gully by hand

Unblocking the soil pipe

Unblocking the soil pipe is an unpleasant job and it's worth hiring a professional cleaning company, especially if the pipe is made of cast iron because it will almost certainly have to be cleared via the vent above the roof.

You can clean a modern plastic stack yourself because there should be a large hinged cleaning eye or other access plugs wherever the branch pipes join the stack. If the stack is inside the house, lay large polythene sheets on the floor and be prepared to mop up trapped sewage when it spills from the pipe.

Unscrew and open the cleaning eye to insert a hired drain auger. Pass the auger into the stack until you locate the obstruction then crank the handle to engage it. Push or pull the auger until you can dislodge the obstruction to clear the trapped water, then hose out the stack. Wash and disinfect the surrounding area.

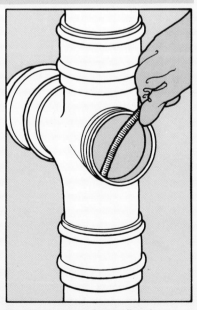
Use a hired auger to clear a soil stack

BLOCKED TOILETS

Unblocking a WC pan

If the water in a WC pan rises when you flush it, there is a blockage in the vicinity of the trap. A partial blockage allows the water level to fall slowly.

Hire a larger version of the sink plunger to force the obstruction into the soil pipe. Position the rubber cap of the plunger well down into the 'U' bend and pump the handle several times. When the blockage clears, the water level will drop suddenly accompanied by an audible gurgling.

If the trap is blocked solidly, hire a special WC auger. Pass the flexible clearing rod as far as possible into the trap, then crank the handle to dislodge the blockage. Wash the auger in hot water and disinfect it before returning the tool to the hire company.

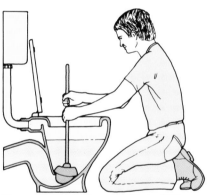
Use a special plunger to pump a blocked WC

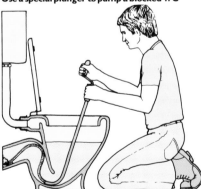
Alternatively, clear it with a WC auger

17

RODDING THE DRAINS

The first sign of a blocked underground drain could be an unpleasant smell from an inspection chamber, but a severe blockage can cause sewage to back up until it begins to overflow from a gully or from beneath the cover of an inspection chamber. Hire a set of drain rods – short, flexible components made of plastic, cane or wire, screwed end to end – to clear a blocked drain. Metal screws or a rubber plunger are threaded onto the rods.

Locating the blockage

Lift the cover from the inspection chamber nearest the house. If it is stuck firmly, or the handles have rusted away, scrape the dirt from around its edges and prise it up with a garden spade.
- If the chamber contains water, check the one nearer the road or boundary. If that chamber is dry, the blockage is between the two chambers.
- If the chamber nearest the road is full, the blockage will be in the interceptor trap or in the pipe beyond leading to the sewer.
- If both chambers are dry and yet either a yard gully or downstairs WC will not empty, check for blockages in the branch drains joining the first inspection chamber.

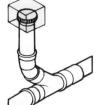

Rodding points
A modern drainage system could be fitted with rodding points to provide access to the drain. They are sealed with small oval or circular covers.

Rodding a drain

Screw two or three rods together and attach a corkscrew fitting to the end. Insert the rods into the drain at the bottom of the inspection chamber in the direction of the suspected blockage. If the chamber is full of water, use the end of a rod to locate an open channel running across the floor, leading to the mouth of the drain.

As you pass the rods along the drain, attach further lengths until you reach the obstruction, then twist the rods clockwise to engage the screw. (Never twist the rods anti-clockwise or they will become detached.) Pull and push the obstruction until it breaks up, allowing the water to flow away. Extract the rods, flush the chamber with a hose and replace the lid.

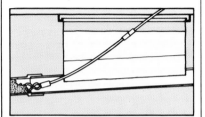

Use a corkscrew fitting to clear a drain

Clearing an interceptor trap

Screw a rubber plunger to the end of a short length of rods and locate the channel leading to the base of the trap. Push the plunger into the opening of the trap, then pump the rods a few times to expel the blockage.

If the water level does not drop after several attempts, try clearing the drain leading to the sewer. Access to this drain is through a cleaning eye above the trap. It will be sealed with a stopper which you will have to dislodge with a drain rod unless it is attached to a chain stapled to the chamber wall. Make sure the stopper doesn't fall into the channel and block the interceptor trap. Rod the drain to the sewer using the corkscrew fitting then hose out the chamber before replacing the stopper and cover.

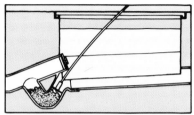

Fit a plunger to rod an interceptor trap

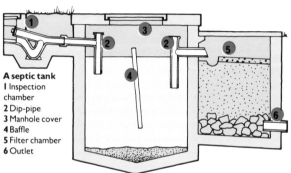

A typical cesspool
1 Inspection chamber
2 Dip-pipe
3 Manhole cover
4 Ventilator
5 Sludge

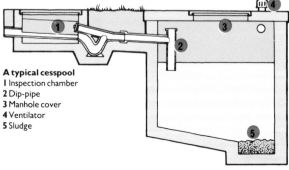

A septic tank
1 Inspection chamber
2 Dip-pipe
3 Manhole cover
4 Baffle
5 Filter chamber
6 Outlet

CESSPOOLS AND SEPTIC TANKS

Houses built in the country or on the outskirts of a town are not always connected to a public sewer. Instead, waste is drained into a cesspool or septic tank. A cesspool is simply a collection point for sewage until it can be pumped out by the local council. A septic tank is a complete waste disposal system in which sewage is broken down by bacterial action before the water is discharged into a local waterway or distributed underground.

Cesspools

Current building regulations stipulate that cesspools should have a minimum capacity of 18 cu m (4,000 gallons) but many existing cesspools accommodate far less, and require emptying perhaps once every two weeks. It would be worth checking on the capacity of a cesspool before you buy a country home to ensure it will cope with your needs. Water authorities estimate **the disposal** of approximately 115 litres (25 gallons) per person per day.

Most cesspools are cylindrical pits

lined with brick or concrete. Modern ones are sometimes prefabricated in glass-reinforced plastic. Access is via a manhole cover.

Septic tanks

The sewage in a septic tank separates slowly, heavy sludge falling to the bottom leaving relatively clear water with a layer of scum floating on the surface. A dip-pipe discharges waste below the surface so that incoming water does not stir up the sewage. Bacterial action takes a minimum of 24 hours so the tank is divided into chambers by baffles to slow down the movement of sewage through the tank.

The partly treated waste passes out of the tank through another dip-pipe into some form of filtration system which allows further bacterial action to take place. It may be another chamber containing a deep filter bed or alternatively, the waste may flow underground through a network of drains which disperses the water over a wide area to filter through the soil.

INSTALLING PIPES

The ability to install a run of pipework, make watertight joints and connect up to fittings are the basic requirements of plumbing. Without those skills, a householder is restricted to simple maintenance. When lead piping was universal, plumbing was a trade requiring years of experience, but modern materials and technology has made it possible for anybody who is prepared to master a few techniques to upgrade and extend household plumbing without having to hire a professional.

Metric and imperial pipes

Copper and stainless steel pipes are now made in metric sizes whereas a lot of pipework already installed in a house will be of the old imperial measurements. If you compare the equivalent dimensions; 15mm – ½in, 22mm – ¾in, and 28mm – 1in; the difference seems obvious, but metric pipe is measured externally while imperial pipe is measured internally. In fact, the difference is very small, but enough to cause some problems when joining one type of pipe to the other.

An exact fit is essential when making soldered joints so imperial to metric adaptors are used for all sizes of pipe. Adaptors are not necessary when joining 15mm and 28mm pipes to their imperial equivalents with compression joints but you will have to use them for joining 22mm to ¾in pipes.

Use 22mm pipes for the main runs and 15mm for most branch pipes. 28mm pipe is for the primary flow and return pipes connected to a boiler (▷).

Electro-chemical action

If you live in a soft water area, take care when joining copper to galvanized steel (iron) pipes or storage tanks. The two metals in combination with a weak acidic solution produce the conditions of an electric cell which gradually dissolve the zinc coating on the steel.

Brass can corrode in a similar way due to the zinc content of the metal. Use corrosion-resistant brass or gunmetal fittings and special copper to steel connectors where these conditions are likely to occur. Check with your water authority for advice.

TYPES OF METAL PLUMBING

Over the years, most household plumbing systems have undergone some form of improvement or alteration. As a result you may find any of a number of metals used, perhaps in combination, depending on the availability of materials at the time it was installed, or the preference of an individual plumber.

COPPER

Half-hard tempered copper tubing is by far the most widely used material for pipework. It is lightweight, solders well and can be bent easily, even by hand with the aid of a bending spring. It is used for both hot and cold water supply as well as central heating systems. Invariably, three sizes of pipe are used for general domestic plumbing: 15mm (½in), 22mm (¾in) and 28mm (1in).

STAINLESS STEEL

Stainless steel tubing is not as common as copper but is available in the same sizes. You may have to order it from a plumbers' merchant. Stainless steel offers few advantages to a DIY plumber. It is harder than copper so cannot be bent as easily and it is difficult to solder. For both reasons, use compression joints to connect stainless steel pipes, but tighten them slightly more than you would when joining copper. Alternatively, use a special adhesive (▷). However, stainless steel does not react adversely with galvanized steel (iron) pipes which may have been installed previously. (See electro-chemical action, left)

LEAD

Lead is never used for new plumbing but thousands of houses still have a lead rising main connected to a modernized system. This is perfectly acceptable, but extensive lead plumbing still in use must be nearing the end of its useful life so replace it whenever the opportunity arises. When drinking water lies in a lead pipe for some time, it absorbs toxins from the metal. If you have a lead pipe supplying your drinking water, always run off a little water before you use any.

GALVANIZED STEEL (IRON)

Galvanized steel was used to provide strong pipework where lead might easily have been damaged. It can still be obtained but there is no longer any point in using it for general plumbing especially as the ends of straight lengths have to be threaded before you can make a joint. Take care when joining copper to existing galvanized steel pipes. (See electro-chemical action, left)

CAST IRON

All old soil pipes are made of cast iron but the metal is very prone to rusting. In fact it is only the relatively thick walls of the pipes that have preserved them for so long. Should you need to replace one, ask for one of the plastic alternatives.

BRASS

Because it machines and casts so well, brass is used to make compression joints, taps, stopcocks and other fittings. Corrosion-resistant brass is used to avoid electro-chemical action between zinc content of brass and copper pipes.

GUNMETAL

Gunmetal connectors are manufactured for joining copper pipework to galvanized steel where standard brass fittings would be corroded.

SEE ALSO

Details for: ▷	
Flow and return	48
Soldered joints	21
Soft water	46
Bending springs	74

● **Gluing stainless steel**
Stainless-steel plumbing can be glued with a special adhesive and activator such as Loctite 638 (Activator 'N') or Permabond A128 ('Speed' primer). Key end of tube and inside of fitting. Spray activator onto both surfaces. After 30 seconds apply a ring of glue to the leading edge of the fitting and to end of tube. Assemble joint and leave it to harden for at least two minutes.

19

METAL PIPE JOINTS

METAL JOINTS AND FITTINGS

As most domestic plumbing is carried out in copper, the methods described on the next few pages are primarily for joining copper pipes. You can use the same techniques for stainless steel plumbing but, because it is harder than copper, you will find it easier to cut the metal with a hacksaw and use an active flux for soldering joints. Join copper to galvanized steel or plastic plumbing with specially designed couplings.

Capillary and compression joints are made to connect pipes at different angles and in various combinations. There are adaptors for joining metric and imperial pipes and for connecting one material to another. You will have to consult manufacturers' catalogues to see every variation, but the examples below illustrate a range of typical joints and fittings.

Compression & capillary joints

It would be impossible to make strong, watertight joints by simply soldering two lengths of copper pipe end to end. Instead, plumbers use capillary or compression joints.

Capillary joints

Capillary joints are made to fit snugly over the ends of the pipe. The very small space between the pipe and sleeve is filled with molten solder which solidifies on cooling to hold the joint together and make it watertight. Capillary joints are neat and inexpensive but, because you need to heat the metal with a blow torch, there is a slight risk of fire when working in confined spaces under floors and in the loft.

Compression joints

Compression joints are very easy to use but are more expensive than capillary joints. They are also more obtrusive, and you will find it impossible to manoeuvre a wrench where space is restricted. When the cap-nut is tightened with a wrench, it compresses a ring of soft metal, known as an olive, to fill the joint between fitting and pipe.

Capillary joints
Solder is introduced to the mouth of the assembled end-feed joint (top) and flows by capillary action into the fitting. The ring pressed into the sleeves of an integral ring fitting (above) contains the exact amount of solder to make a perfect joint.

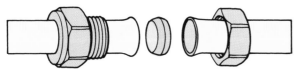

Manipulative compression joint
The ends of the pipes are flared to accept a soft copper cone. When the nut is tightened, the cone is compressed to seal the joint.

Non-manipulative compression joint
This is the simplest and most widely used compression joint. The end of each pipe is cut square before the joint is assembled.

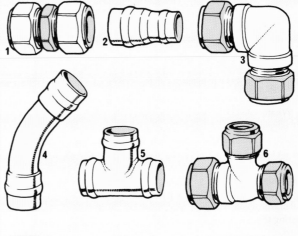

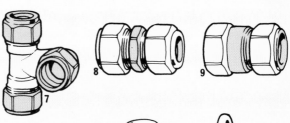

Straight connectors
To join two pipes end to end in a straight line.
1 For pipes of equal diameter – *compression joint*
2 Reducer to connect 22mm (¾in) and 15mm (½in) pipes – *capillary joint*

Bends or elbows
To join two pipes at 90 degrees or 45 degrees.
3 90 degree elbow – *compression joint*
4 45 degree elbow – *capillary joint*

Tees
To join three pipes.
5 Equal tee to join three pipes of the same diameter – *capillary joint*
6 Unequal tee to reduce size of pipe run and join a branch pipe – *compression joint*
7 Off-set tee joins branch pipe to one side of main pipe run – *compression joint*

Adaptors
To join dissimilar pipes.
8 Straight coupling to join 22mm and ¾in pipes – *compression joint*
9 Copper to galvanized steel connector – *compression joint* for copper, *threaded female coupling* for steel

Fittings
Identical jointing systems are used to connect fittings.
10 Tank connector joins pipes to cisterns – *compression joint*
11 Tap connector with threaded nut for connecting supply pipe to tap – *capillary joint*
12 Bib tap wall plate for fixing tap on outside wall – *compression joint* for supply pipe, *threaded female connector* for tap
13 Bib tap has threaded tail to fit wall plate
14 Gate valve to fit in straight pipe run – *compression joint*
15 Drain cock to empty a pipe run – *compression joint*

Soldering pipe joints is very simple once you have had a little practice. The fittings are relatively cheap so try out the techniques before you install actual pipework. Your basic equipment is a gas torch to apply heat, some flux to clean the metal and solder to make the joint.

CUTTING METAL PIPE

Calculate the length of pipe you need, allowing enough to fit into the sleeve of the joint at each end. Whatever type of joint you use, it is essential to cut the end of every length of pipe square.

To ensure a perfectly square cut each time, use a tube cutter. Align the cutting wheel with your mark, and adjust the handle of the tool to clamp the rollers against the pipe (1). Rotate the tool around the pipe, adjusting the handle after each revolution to make the cutter bite deeper into the metal.

Use the pointed reamer on the end of the tool to clean the burr from inside the cut pipe (2). A tube cutter makes a clean cut on the outside of the pipe automatically.

If you want to use a hacksaw, make sure the cut is square by wrapping a piece of paper with a straight edge around the pipe. Align the wrapped edge and use it to guide the saw blade (3). Remove the burr, inside and out, with a file.

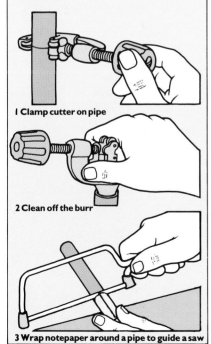

1 Clamp cutter on pipe

2 Clean off the burr

3 Wrap notepaper around a pipe to guide a saw

Gas torches

To heat the metal sufficiently to make a good soldered joint, most plumbers use a gas torch. Gas, liquefied under pressure, is contained in a disposable metal canister. When the control valve of the torch is opened, gas is vapourized to combine with air to make a highly combustible mixture. Once ignited, the flame is adjusted until it burns with a clear, blue colour.

Many professional plumbers use a propane torch connected by a hose to a metal gas bottle. The average householder does not need such expensive equipment, but if you happen to own a propane torch, perhaps for car repairs, you can use the same tool to solder plumbing joints.

Using integral ring joints

Clean the ends of each pipe and the inside of the joint sleeves with wire wool or abrasive paper until the metal is shiny. Brush flux onto the cleaned metal and push the pipes into the joint, twisting them to spread the flux evenly. Make sure each pipe is up against the integral stop in the joint. Wipe off excess flux with a cloth.

If you are using elbows or tees, mark the pipe and joint with a pencil to make sure they do not get misaligned during the soldering.

Slip a ceramic tile or plumbers' fibreglass mat behind the joint to protect any flammable materials, then apply the flame of a gas torch over the area of the joint to heat it evenly (1).

Using end-feed joints

Clean and assemble an end-feed joint like an integral ring type, then heat the area of the joint evenly. When the flux begins to bubble, remove the flame and touch the end of the solder wire to two

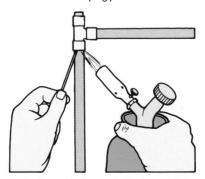

1 Heat the joint to melt the captive solder

2 Introduce solder to a heated end-feed joint

Solder and flux

Solder is a soft alloy of tin and lead manufactured with a melting point lower than that of the metal it is joining. Plumbers' solder is sold as wound wire.

Copper must be spotlessly clean and grease-free to produce a properly soldered joint. Even when you have cleaned it mechanically with wire wool, copper begins to oxidize immediately, so a chemical cleaner known as flux is painted onto the metal to provide a barrier against oxidation until the solder is applied. A non-corrosive flux in the form of a paste is the best one to use, but for stainless steel use a highly efficient active flux but wash it off with warm water after the joint is made or the metal will corrode.

When a bright ring of solder appears at each end of the joint, remove the flame and allow the metal to cool for a couple of minutes before disturbing it.

Repairing a weeping joint
When you fill a new installation with water for the first time, check every joint to make sure it is watertight. If you notice water 'weeping' from a soldered joint, drain the pipe and allow it to dry. Heat the joint and apply some fresh solder to the edge of each mouth. If it leaks a second time, heat the joint until you can pull it apart with gloved hands. Use a new **joint,** or clean and flux all surfaces and reuse the same joint as an end-feed fitting.

or three points around the mouth of each sleeve (2). You will know that the joint is full of solder when a bright ring appears around each sleeve. Allow it to cool. Mend a weeping joint as above.

Gas torches
A gas torch is used to heat soldered joints. A simple torch (top) is available from any DIY outlet. The propane torch (above) is used by professional plumbers.

MAKING COMPRESSION JOINTS

Using non-manipulative joints is so straightforward that you will be able to make watertight joints without any previous experience. There is no advantage in using a manipulative joint unless it will be under tension.

Using non-manipulative joints

Cut the ends of each pipe square and clean them, along with the olives, with wire wool. Dismantle the joint and slip a cap-nut onto a pipe followed by an olive (**1**). Look carefully to see if the sloping sides of the olive are equal in length. If one is longer than the other, that side should face away from the nut.

Push the pipe firmly into the joint body (**2**), twisting it slightly to ensure it is firmly against the integral stop. Slide the olive up to the body then hand tighten the nut.

The olive must be compressed the right amount to ensure a watertight joint. As a guide, use a pencil to mark one face of the nut and the opposing face on the joint body then, holding the body steady with a spanner, use another to turn the nut one complete revolution (**3**). Assemble the other half of the joint in the same way.

To make absolutely sure the joint is watertight, some plumbers prefer to smear a little jointing compound onto the olive before tightening the nut, but a properly tightened compression joint should be watertight without it.

Repairing a weeping joint
Having filled the pipe with water, check each joint for leaks. Make one further quarter turn on any nut that appears to be weeping.

Crushing an olive by overtightening a compression joint will cause it to leak. Drain the pipe and dismantle the joint. Cut through the damaged olive with a junior hacksaw taking care not to damage the pipe. Remake the joint with a new olive, restore the supply of water and check for leaks once more.

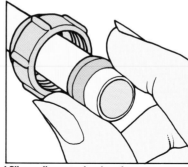

1 Slip an olive onto the pipe after a cap-nut

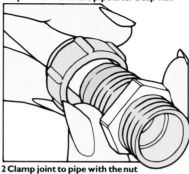

2 Clamp joint to pipe with the nut

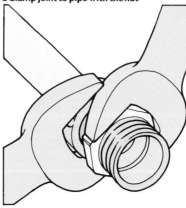

3 Tighten the joint with two spanners

Using manipulative joints

Whatever type of manipulative compression joint you use, the ends of the tubing must be shaped (manipulated) to fit the joint. There are special flaring tools to produce the effect, or drive a steel drift into the end of the pipe. Follow the manufacturer's instructions for individual joints, but the following example demonstrates the principle.

Having cut and cleaned the pipes, slip the cap-nut onto one tube and the joint body onto the other. Insert the drift into one pipe and strike it with a hammer until the cone of the drift flares the pipe (**1**). Flare the other pipe in the same way. Sandwich a copper compression ring or 'cone' between the flared pipes and smear the area with jointing compound. Hand-tighten the cap-nut then use two spanners to complete the joint.

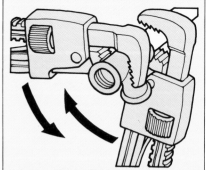

1 Manipulative joint
Flare the pipe by driving a metal drift into one end.

MAKING COPPER TO STEEL CONNECTIONS

Galvanized steel pipe is connected by threaded joints so if you plan to extend old pipework using the same material, you will need a pipe die to cut the threads on the end of each length of new pipe. You can hire the tool but it would be simpler to continue the run in copper using an adaptor to connect one system to another. One end of the adaptor has a capillary or compression joint for the copper pipework. The other end has a male or female threaded connector for the galvanized steel.

Use two stilson wrenches to unscrew the joint on the old pipework where you intend to connect up to copper. Grip the joint with one wrench and the pipe with the other, pushing and pulling in the direction the jaws face (**1**). If the joint is stiff, use penetrating oil or play the flame of a gas torch along it.

Threaded connections leak unless they are made watertight with plumbers' hemp or PTFE tape. To use hemp, smear some jointing compound (a waterproofing paste sold by plumbers' merchants) around the male thread. Tease out a short length of hemp and wrap it clockwise around the thread. Leave about one third of the thread free at the end of the pipe to engage the connector accurately before it encounters the hemp (**2**). Tighten the joint with a spanner.

PTFE tape is bound over the threads instead of the hemp. No jointing compound is required. Wrap the tape clockwise two or three times around the pipe (**3**), engage and tighten the nut.

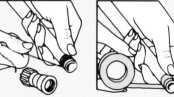

1 Unscrew a joint with two stilson wrenches

2 Wrap with hemp   3 Or use PTFE tape

MAKING COPPER TO LEAD CONNECTIONS

When lead plumbing is replaced with copper, the new pipework is usually connected to a short section of the original lead rising main. This is now the only time when a lead to copper joint is required, and it occurs so infrequently that it makes sense to hire a professional to make the rather specialized joint.

The joint is achieved by soldering a short length of copper pipe, to which the new rising main will be connected, into the end of the lead pipe. The lead is flared by driving a hardwood cone into it or by inserting a metal rod in the end and revolving it to force the edge of the pipe outwards (1).

A chamfer is filed around the jointing edge of the copper pipe then the tube is cleaned with wire wool. The lead is scraped, inside and out, back to clean, shiny metal.

To prevent the solder sticking to either metal outside the area of the joint, first chalk then 'plumbers' black' is applied to each pipe about 35mm (1½in) away from the joint (2).

The copper is tinned with solder before it is inserted into the pipe, then a length of dowel is passed through both tubes to align them. A nail driven through the wood stops the dowel falling into the pipe.

Heat is applied to the area of the joint with a gas torch, then tallow is smeared over the joint itself. A heavy stick of solder, composed of 2 parts lead: 1 part tin, is applied to the hot metal, and built up to a generous thickness, filling the flared end of the lead pipe (3). The soft solder is smoothed by hand with a tallow-soaked felt pad known as a 'mole' (4).

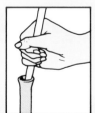

1 Flare the lead

2 Apply plumbers' black

3 Melt stick of solder

4 Smooth with a mole

BENDING PIPES

You can change the direction of a pipe run by using an elbow joint but there are occasions when bending the pipe itself will produce a neater or more accurate result. If you want to carry a pipe over a small obstruction, like another pipe for instance, a slight kink in the pipe will be less of an obstruction to the flow of water than two joints within a few centimetres of each other. It is also cheaper. You might want to run pipes into a window alcove where the walls meet at an unusual angle. Bending the pipes accurately will allow you to fit the pipes neatly against the walls of the alcove.

Using a bending spring

A bending spring is the cheapest and easiest tool for making bends in small pipe runs. It is a hardened steel coil spring which supports the walls of copper tube to stop it kinking. Most bending springs are made to fit inside the pipe but some slide over the tube.

Slide the spring into the tube to support the area you want to bend. Hold the tube against your knee and bend it to the required angle (1).

A bent tube grips the spring but if you slip a screwdriver into the ring at one end and twist it anti-clockwise, it reduces the diameter of the spring so that you can pull it out. If you make a bend some distance from the end of a tube, you can't withdraw the bending spring in the normal way. Either use an external spring, or tie a length of twine to the ring and lightly grease the spring with petroleum jelly before you insert it. Slightly overbend the tube and open it out to the correct angle to release the spring, then pull it out with the twine.

Using a pipe bender

Although you can hire bending springs to fit the larger pipes, it isn't easy to bend 22mm or 28mm (¾ or 1in) tube over your knee. It is well worth hiring a pipe bender.

Hold the pipe against the radiused former and insert the straight former to support it. Pull both levers towards each other to make the bend, then open up the bender to remove the pipe.

Getting the bends in the right place

To make sure a bend is in the right place along a pipe, bend the tube before you cut it to length.

It is difficult to position more than two bends along one length of pipe. If you want to fit an alcove for instance, bend two tubes, one to fit each side, then cut the tubes where they overlap and insert a joint.

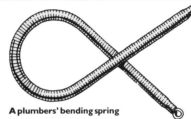

A plumbers' bending spring

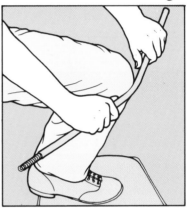

1 Bend the pipe against your knee

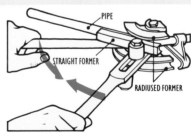

PIPE
STRAIGHT FORMER
RADIUSED FORMER

Use a pipe bender for larger tubing

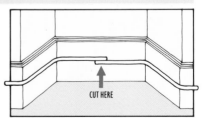

CUT HERE

Bend two separate tubes to fit an alcove

Supporting pipe runs
Place a plastic or metal clip every metre (yard) along a horizontal run of 15mm (½in) pipe, but increase the spacing to every 1.5m (4ft 6in) on a vertical run. For larger pipes, increase the spacing a little more.

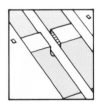

Notching floorboards
When you run pipes under floorboards, notch each joist to receive the pipe. Cut the notch to align with the centre of a floorboard and drive a nail on each side when replacing the board.

PLASTIC PLUMBING

The introduction of plastics is probably the most innovative development in plumbing since copper was first used. Plastic plumbing is cheap, lightweight and extremely easy to construct. It does not freeze, corrode or adversely affect other materials, and depending on the type of plastic, it can be used for hot and cold water including central heating pipework. It is already used universally for waste systems and is becoming increasingly popular for supply pipes.

Being a comparatively recent development, plastic plumbing is not yet standardized. As a result, it is advisable to use one manufacturer's range of equipment and materials to ensure that every component is compatible.

Some plastics are still being tested by water authorities, and may not be officially approved for certain applications. Use manufacturers' catalogues as a guide or seek the advice of your supplier.

Most plastic systems can be connected to existing metal pipe with special adaptors.

Plastic pipe: standard sizes

Plastic pipes are made to more or less standard sizes, but there may be slight variation from one manufacturer's stock to another. As with metal pipework, most metric dimensions refer to the outside diameter of the tube and imperial dimensions to the inside, but not all manufacturers specify their pipes in the same way. Check that pipes and fittings are compatible with existing plumbing before you buy them. The following list is a guide to the available sizes of plastic pipe.

PLASTIC PIPEWORK	
General pipework	15mm (½in); 22mm (¾in); 28mm (1in)
Overflow pipes	21mm (¾in)
Wash basin waste pipes	36mm (1¼in)
Bath/sink waste pipes	43mm (1½in)
Soil pipe	100mm (4in)

PLASTIC JOINTS AND FITTINGS

Most plastic joints and fittings are similar to those used for metal plumbing but in addition, there are easy-flow bends and tees for drainage systems. These joints frequently have cleaning eyes or access plugs for removing blockages in the pipe. Joints and pipes are normally made from the same material, but there are several specialized connectors with metal couplings for joining plastic plumbing to taps, valves and existing metal plumbing.

You will have to browse through different manufacturers' catalogues to see the huge variety of plastic joints for both supply and waste systems, but the selection illustrated below shows the main categories of joint with examples of the different types of coupling.

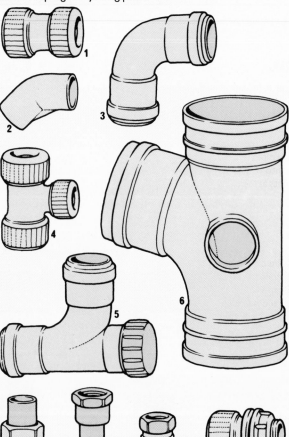

Straight connectors
To join two pipes end to end in a straight line.
1 For pipes of equal diameter – *push-fit*: supply

Bends or elbows
To join two pipes at an angle.
2 45 degree elbow – *solvent weld*: supply
3 Easy-flow bend – *push-fit*: waste

Tees
To join three pipes.
4 Unequal tee to join 15mm (½in) branch pipe to main pipe run – *push-fit*: supply
5 Swept tee with access plug – *push-fit*: waste
6 Branch tee to WC – *solvent weld*: soil pipe

Adaptors
To join dissimilar pipes.
7 Plastic to copper connector – *solvent weld* and *compression joint*: supply
8 Plastic to galvanized steel connector – *push-fit* and *threaded female coupling*: supply

Fittings
Specialized connections are available to join plastic plumbing to fittings. Each manufacturer will supply items like taps and valves to match their particular range.
9 Tap connector with threaded nut for connecting supply pipe to tail of tap – *solvent weld*: supply
10 Tank connector joins pipes to storage cisterns – *push-fit*: supply
11 Stop cock – *push-fit*: supply
12 Sink trap – *compression joint*: waste

JOINING PLASTIC PIPES

Plastics are complex materials, each with its own properties. A technique or material that is suitable for joining one plastic might be quite useless for another. To make sure joints are watertight, it is important to follow each manufacturer's instructions carefully, and to use the solvents and lubricants they recommend. The following examples illustrate the common methods used to connect plastic plumbing.

Solvent weld joints

Lengths of pipe are linked by simple socketed connectors. As they are assembled, a solvent is introduced to the joint which dissolves the surfaces of the mating components. As the solvent evaporates, the joint and pipes are literally fused together into one piece of plastic. Solvent weld joints are used for supply and waste pipes.

Push-fit joints – waste systems

Because a waste system is never under pressure, a pipe run can be constructed by simply pushing plain pipes into the sockets of the joints. A captive rubber seal in each socket holds the pipe in place and makes the joint watertight.

Push-fit joints – supply systems

Polybutylene pipes are connected with a unique push-fit joint. When the pipe is inserted, an 'O' ring seals in the water in the normal way, but a metal grab ring behind the seal has one-way barbed teeth to prevent the pipe being pulled out again. The joints can be dismantled, but only by removing the retaining cap and crushing the grab ring. The joints are more obtrusive than welded types but the speed and simplicity with which you can assemble them more than compensates.

Compression joints

So that they can be dismantled easily, sink, bath and basin traps are often connected to the pipework by compression joints incorporating a rubber ring or washer to make the joint watertight.

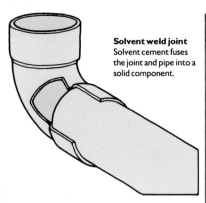

Solvent weld joint
Solvent cement fuses the joint and pipe into a solid component.

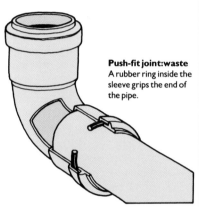

Push-fit joint: waste
A rubber ring inside the sleeve grips the end of the pipe.

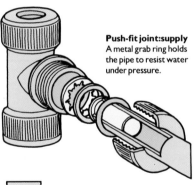

Push-fit joint: supply
A metal grab ring holds the pipe to resist water under pressure.

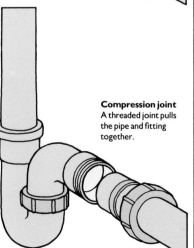

Compression joint
A threaded joint pulls the pipe and fitting together.

TYPES OF PLASTIC

The technology of plastics is such that new or modified materials are being introduced all the time, but the plastics described below are widely available.

Unplasticized polyvinyl chloride

UPVC
A hard, rigid plastic used for waste systems and cold water supply.

Modified polyvinyl chloride

PVC
A similar plastic to UPVC but it is slightly more flexible and therefore shock resistant.

Chlorinated polyvinyl chloride

CPVC
A versatile plastic suitable for hot and cold water supply. It can even withstand the temperatures required for central heating systems.

Polypropylene

PP
A slightly flexible plastic with a somewhat greasy feel. It is used for hot and cold waste systems but expands when heated. It is impossible to glue PP so it's never welded with solvent.

Acrylonitrile butadiene styrene

ABS
A very tough plastic equally suited to hot and cold waste.

Polybutylene

PB
A tough, flexible plastic used for hot and cold water supply – even central heating. Available in standard lengths or continuous coils.

SEE ALSO

Details for: ▷

Solvent joints	27
Push-fit joints	26-27

25

MAKING JOINTS IN PLASTIC PIPES

You should follow the detailed advice supplied with any specific make of pipe or fitting, but the instructions below and on the facing page demonstrate the basic methods used to connect plastic pipework. Do not inhale solvent fumes, and especially avoid smoking when welding joints. Some solvents give off fumes which become toxic when inhaled through a cigarette. Keep solvents away from children. Work carefully to avoid spilling solvent cement as it will etch the surface of the pipework and certain other plastics as well.

JOINING PUSH-FIT WASTE PIPES

Cut the pipe to length and chamfer the end as for solvent weld joints. Wipe the inside of the socket with the recommended cleaner and lubricate the pipe with a little of the silicone lubricant supplied with it.

Push the pipe into the joint right up to the stop and mark the edge of the socket on the pipe with a pencil (1).

Withdraw the pipe about 10mm (⅜in) (2) to allow the pipe to expand when subjected to hot water.

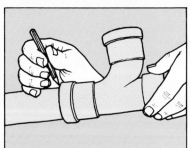

1 Mark the edge of the socket on the pipe

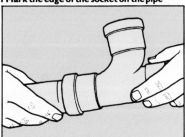

2 Withdraw the pipe about 10mm (⅜in)

Repairing a weeping joint
If a push-fit joint is leaking, the rubber seal has been pushed out of position, probably because the socket is out of line with the pipe. Dismantle the joint and check the condition of the seal.

6 Expansion loop
Build a loop into a long pipe run to allow for expansion using short lengths of tube and elbows.

Making solvent weld joints

Cut the pipe to length with a saw allowing for the depth of the joint socket. When working with large diameter pipes, make sure your cut is square by winding a piece of note paper around the tube, aligning the wrapped edge carefully as a guide for the saw (1).

Revolve the pipe away from you as you cut it. Smooth the cut edge with a file.

Chamfer the pipe with a file to make it easier to push into the socket (2).

Welding the joint
Push the pipe into the socket to test the fit then mark the end of the joint on the pipe with a pencil (3). This will act as a guide for applying the solvent. You must key the outside of the pipe up to this line, and the inside of the socket, with fine abrasive paper before using some solvents. Check the manufacturer's instructions.

When using elbows and tees, scratch the pipe and joint with a knife (4) before dismantling to align them correctly when you reassemble the components.

Use a clean rag to wipe the surface of pipe and fitting with the recommended spirit cleaner.

Paint solvent evenly onto both components (5) and immediately push home the socket. (Some manufacturers recommend that you twist the joint to spread the solvent.) Align the joint properly and leave it for 15 seconds.

The pipe is ready for use with cold water after one hour. Do not pass hot water through the system until at least four hours has elapsed, preferably longer, according to manufacturer's recommendations.

Allowing for expansion
Plastic pipes expand when subjected to hot water but this is only a problem over a long, straight run.
● If a waste run exceeds 1.8m (6ft), incorporate an expansion coupling with a push-fit rubber seal at one end,.
● For supply pipes over 10m (33ft) in length, form an expansion loop in the run by joining three 150mm (3in) lengths of pipe with elbows (6).

Repairing a weeping joint
If a joint leaks when the system is filled with water, drain it again and allow it to dry out. Apply a little more solvent cement to the mouth of the socket allowing it to flow into the joint by capillary action.

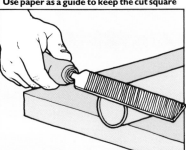

1 Use paper as a guide to keep the cut square

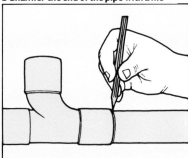

2 Chamfer the end of the pipe with a file

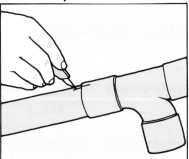

3 Assemble the joint and mark the socket

4 Scratch pipe and joint to realign them

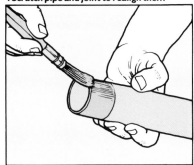

5 Paint solvent up to pencil mark

MAKING JOINTS IN PLASTIC PIPES

Joining push-fit supply pipes

Cut polybutylene pipe to length with special shears supplied by the manufacturer (1), or use a sharp craft knife. As long as the cut is reasonably square, the joint will be watertight.

Push a metal support sleeve into the pipe (2), then use a fingertip to smear a little silicone lubricant around the end of the pipe and inside the socket (3).

Push the prepared pipe firmly into the socket a full 25mm (1in) (4). As the joint can revolve freely around the pipe after connection without breaking the seal, there is no problem when aligning tees and elbows with other pipe runs.

1 Cut pipe to length

2 Insert metal sleeve

3 Apply lubricant

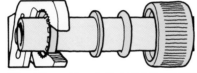

4 Push pipe into joint

Dismantling a joint

If you need to dismantle a joint to alter a system, release the cap with mole grips (▷) and unscrew it by hand. Pull out the pipe, slide the rubber ring and washer along the pipe then crush the metal grab ring with pliers (5) to remove it.

Drop a new grab ring into the socket – teeth facing into the fitting – and replace first the washer, then the rubber ring.

Screw back the cap hand-tight then use mole grips to turn it 2mm (1/8in) further. Overtightening will render the joint ineffective.

Connect to the pipe as described above. Never attempt to assemble the fitting like a compression joint or it will blow out under pressure.

Repairing a weeping joint
The only reason why a supply push-fit joint should leak is the failure to push home the pipe fully.

5 Crush the metal grab ring to dismantle joint

Bending plastic pipes

It isn't practical to bend plastic wastepipes especially when you can use easy-flow joints instead.

It is possible to bend a rigid supply pipe by heating it gently. Pass the flame of a gas torch over the area you wish to bend. Keep the flame moving and revolve the pipe all the time. When the pipe is soft enough, bend it by hand on a flat surface (1) and hold it still until the plastic hardens again.

Polybutylene pipe can be bent cold to a minimum radius of eight times the pipe diameter. Use a pipe clip at each side of the bend to hold the curve, or use the manufacturer's special clamp (2). Because the pipe is flexible, long gentle curves can be made by simply threading it around obstacles. Running this type of pipe under floorboards is very easy.

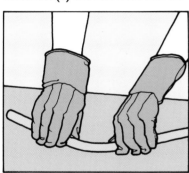

1 Bend the softened pipe on a flat surface

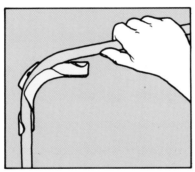

2 Hook flexible pipe into a metal clamp

MAKING COMPRESSION JOINTS TO TRAPS

With some traps, a short threaded pipe is located in the outlet of the trap and secured by a large compression nut. The other end of the pipe is connected to the rest of the waste system with a push-fit or solvent weld joint.

Other traps connect directly to a plain wastepipe. Slip the threaded nut onto the pipe followed by the washer and then the rubber ring.

Push the pipe into the socket of the trap and tighten the compression nut.

CONNECTING PLASTIC TO METAL PLUMBING

To connect most plastic pipes to copper or galvanized steel plumbing, use special adaptor couplings (▷).

To join polybutylene pipe to copper, insert the usual support sleeve then use a standard brass compression joint. Alternatively, you can joint copper to a polybutylene run using the push-fit joint. Cut and deburr the copper pipe carefully and lubricate it before pushing it into the joint.

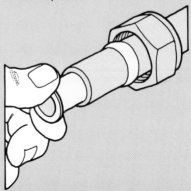

Joining plastic pipe with compression fitting
Insert support sleeve before tightening joint.

SUPPORTING PIPE RUNS

Plastic pipework should be supported with clips or saddles similar to those used for metal pipe, but because it is more flexible, you will have to space the clips closer together. Check with manufacturers' literature for exact dimensions.

If you plan to surface-run flexible pipes, consider ducting or boxing-in because it's difficult to make a really neat installation.

REPLACING A WC SUITE

When remodelling a bathroom, you may decide to relace an old-style, high-level WC cistern with one of the more compact and less obtrusive low-level versions. In many cases this can be achieved without having to renew the pan at the same time, but if that too is old and unsightly, or if the joint with the soil pipe is leaking, take the opportunity to install a completely new suite. If you connect to the existing branch of the soil pipe, it is a relatively simple operation, but if you plan to move the WC or even install a second convenience elsewhere, you will have to break into the main soil pipe itself or run the waste directly into the underground drainage system. In either case, hire a professional plumber to make the installation.

Choosing the equipment

There was a time when more or less every WC looked identical and worked in the same way, but you have now a choice of compact and colourful appliances which perform their functions more quietly and efficiently than their predecessors.

Types of cistern

Most WCs are fitted with a direct action cistern (◁) but this basic design is available in various models.

High-level cistern
If you simply want to replace an existing high-level cistern without having to modify the plumbing, comparable cisterns are still widely available.

Standard low-level cistern
Most people prefer a cistern mounted on the wall just above the WC pan. A short flush pipe from the base of the cistern connects to the flushing horn on the rear of the pan, while inlet and overflow pipes can be fitted to either side of the cistern. Most low-level cisterns are made from the same vitreous china as the pan.

Compact low-level cistern
Where space is limited, use a plastic cistern which is only 114mm (4½in)

from front to back. This type of cistern is operated by a push-down knob on top.

Concealed cistern
A low-level cistern can be concealed behind panelling. Supply and overflow connections are identical to other cisterns but the flushing lever is mounted on the face of the panel. These plastic cisterns are utilitarian in character with no concession to fashion or style, and are therefore relatively inexpensive. You must provide access for servicing.

Close-coupled cisterns
A close-coupled cistern is bolted directly to the pan forming an integral unit. Both the inlet and overflow connections are made at the base of the cistern. An internal standpipe rises vertically from the overflow connection to protrude above the level of the water in the cistern.

Types of WC pan

When you visit a showroom you are confronted with many apparently different WC pans to choose from, but in fact, there are two basic patterns, a washdown or syphonic pan.

Siphonic pans
Siphonic pans need no heavy fall of water to cleanse them and are much quieter as a result. A single trap pan has a narrow outlet immediately after the bend to slow down the flow of water from the pan. The body of water expels air from the outlet to promote the siphonic action. A double trap pan is more sophisticated and exceptionally

quiet. A small vent pipe connects the space between two traps to the inlet running between the cistern and pan. As water flows along the inlet, it sucks air from the trap system through the vent pipe. A vacuum is formed between the traps, and water in the pan is forced by atmospheric pressure into the soil pipe.

Washdown pans
If your existing pan is old enough to need replacing, it will be a standard washdown model. It is the most straightforward and least expensive pan. The contents are washed out by the water falling from the cistern.

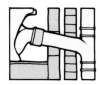

Space for a WC
You will need a space in front of the pan of at least 600mm (2ft) square.

Floor exit trap
Use an 'S' trap when the soil pipe passes through the floor.

Wall exit trap
Use a 'P' trap when the pipe passes through the wall behind the pan.

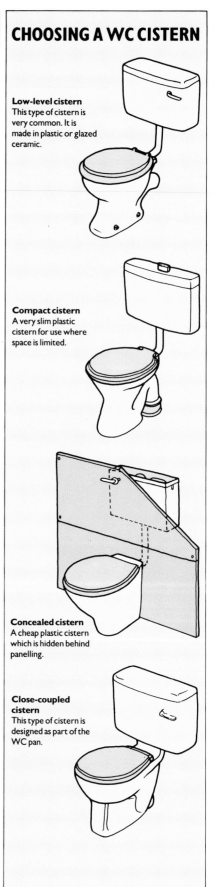

Low-level cistern
This type of cistern is very common. It is made in plastic or glazed ceramic.

Compact cistern
A very slim plastic cistern for use where space is limited.

Concealed cistern
A cheap plastic cistern which is hidden behind panelling.

Close-coupled cistern
This type of cistern is designed as part of the WC pan.

CHOOSING A WC PAN

Washdown pan
The common WC pan with a simple 'S' or 'P' trap filled with water.

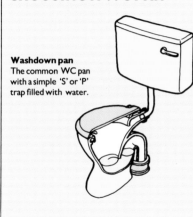

Single trap siphonic pan
The narrow outlet behind the trap slows down the flow of water to produce the siphonic action.

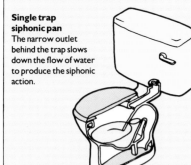

Double trap siphonic pan
Air is sucked out from between the two traps to make a vacuum.

Wall-hung pan
A wall-mounted pan, connected to a concealed cistern, leaves the floor clear for cleaning. Unless it is built into the masonry, the pan is supported by a metal bracket/stand.

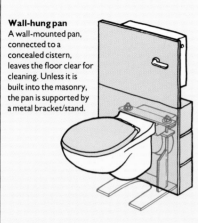

REMOVING THE OLD WC

Cut off the water supply (▷) then flush the cistern to empty it. If you are merely renewing a cistern, you will have to disconnect the supply and overflow pipes with a wrench and loosen the large nut connecting the flush pipe to the base of the cistern. These connections are often corroded and painted, so it is easier to hacksaw through the pipes close to the connections if you intend to replace the entire suite.

Having lifted the cistern off its support brackets, try freeing the fixing screws. In all probability, they will be corroded, so lever the brackets off the wall with a crow bar.

Cut the overflow pipe from the wall with a cold chisel. Repair the plaster when you decorate the bathroom.

If the old pan is screwed to a wooden floor, it will probably have a 'P' trap connected to a nearly horizontal branch soil pipe. Remove the floor fixing screws and scrape out the old putty around the pipe joint. Attempt to free the pan by pulling it towards you while rocking it slightly from side to side.

If the joint is fixed firmly, smash the pan outlet just in front of the soil pipe with a club hammer (1). Protect your eyes with goggles. Stuff rags into the soil pipe to prevent debris falling into it, then chip out the remains of the pan outlet with a cold chisel (2). Work carefully to preserve the soil pipe.

Smash an 'S' trap in the same way, and if the pan is cemented to a solid floor, drive a cold chisel under its base to break the seal. Chop out the broken fragments as before and clean up the floor with a cold chisel.

SEE ALSO

Details for: ▷	
Turning off water	8
WC cistern	12
Chain-link cutter	73

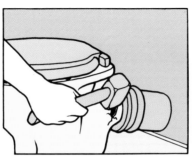
1 Break the outlet of the pan with a hammer

2 Use a cold chisel to cut out the remnants

Cutting the soil pipe

If you break the soil pipe while chipping out the pan outlet, cut the pipe square with a hired chain-link pipe cutter. Clamp the chain of cutters around the pipe and work the shaft back and forth to sever it. Ratchet-action cutters enable you to work in a confined space. When you buy a push-fit pan connector (see below), make sure it is long enough to reach the severed pipe.

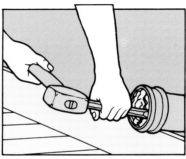

Pan to soil pipe connection

Before you install the new suite, choose a push-fit flexible connector to join the pan to the soil pipe. Connectors of different angles are available to suit any situation, even if the two elements are slightly misaligned. You can even choose a colour to match the suite. Make a note of the following dimensions when selecting a connector: the external diameter of pan outlet; the internal diameter of soil pipe; the distance between the outlet and pipe when the pan is installed.

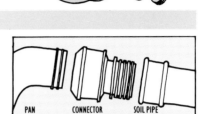
PAN   CONNECTOR   SOIL PIPE

OFF-SET   CRANKED   BENT

Push-fit flexible pan connectors

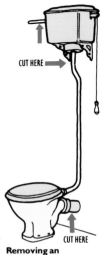

CUT HERE

CUT HERE

Removing an appliance
If fittings are corroded, remove the appliance by cutting the flush pipe, overflow and pan outlet.

Cutting a soil pipe
Use a chain-link cutter to sever a broken soil pipe.

INSTALLING A NEW WC SUITE

To install a new WC, begin by pushing the plastic connector onto the pan outlet. Check that the inside of the soil pipe is clean and smooth. Smear a rough surface with a lubricant supplied by the manufacturer then push the pan and connector firmly into the soil pipe.

Don't fix the pan at this stage, but if the floor is made of concrete, you will have to drill holes and plug the fixing holes. Level the pan using a spirit level, adjusting it with scraps of veneer or vinyl floor covering. (Trim them with a knife when the installation is complete.)

Stand a close-coupled cistern on the pan, or connect the flush pipe and hold the cistern against the wall to mark the fixing holes. Fix the cistern to the wall with non-corroding screws and washers making sure it is level, then tighten the

flush pipe connection under the cistern.

Screw the pan to the floor, tightening the screws carefully in rotation to avoid cracking the pan.

Run the new 15mm (½in) supply pipe to the float valve (◁), fit a tap connector and tighten it with a wrench.

Use a tank connector (◁) to attach the 21mm (¾in) overflow pipe. Drill a hole through the nearest outside wall where an overflow will be detected prompty. Slope the pipe a few degrees and let it project from the outer face of the wall at least 150mm (6in).

When there is no external wall nearby, you can run the WC overflow pipe to a special combined waste and overflow unit on the bath (◁).

Turn on the supply of water and adjust the float valve (◁).

Plumbing a WC
1 Bent plastic tank connector
2 21mm (¾in) overflow
3 Cistern
4 Float valve
5 Tap connector
6 15mm (½in) supply pipe
7 Flush pipe connector
8 Flush pipe
9 Push-fit flexible connector
10 WC pan outlet
11 Flexible outlet connector
12 Soil pipe

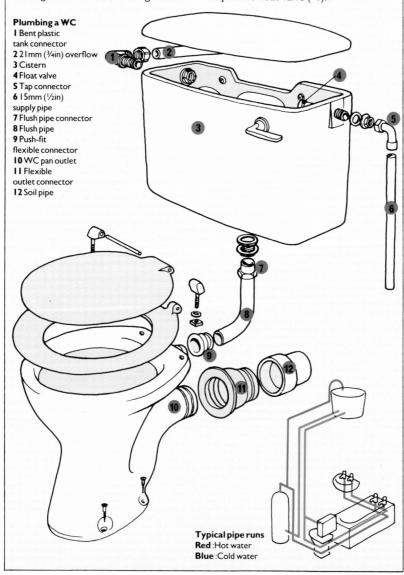

Typical pipe runs
Red:Hot water
Blue:Cold water

Small bore waste system

The siting of a WC is normally limited by the need to use a conventional 100mm (4in) soil pipe, and to provide sufficient fall to discharge the waste into the soil stack. By using an electrically driven pump and shredder, you can discharge WC waste through a 22mm (¾in) pipe up to 50m (55yd) away from the stack. The shredder will even pump vertically to a maximum of 4m (4yd). You can run the small-bore pipework through the narrow space between a floor and ceiling (◁). Consequently, a WC can be installed as part of an en-suite bathroom, under the stairs or even in a basement providing the space is adequately ventilated.

The unit, which accepts any conventional 'P' trap WC pan, is activated automatically by flushing the cistern and switches off about 18 seconds later. It must be wired to a fused connection unit, but via a suitable flex outlet if installed in a bathroom (◁). The wastepipe is connected to the soil stack using any standard 36mm (1¼in) waste boss (◁) so long as the manufacturer supplies a 22-36mm (¾-1¼in) adaptor. A WC waste must be connected to the stack at least 200mm (8in) above other waste connections.

Check that the system is approved by your local water authority before installation.

Small bore waste system for a WC
The shredding unit fits neatly behind a 'P' trap WC pan. When it is situated in a bathroom, the unit must be wired to a flex outlet as shown above (◁), otherwise it can be connected directly to a fused connection unit (◁).

FITTING A WASH BASIN

Whether you are modifying existing plumbing or running new pipework to a different location, fitting a wash basin in a bathroom or guest room presents few difficulties so long as you give some thought to how you will run the waste to the vertical stack. The waste must have a minimum fall or slope of 6mm (1/4in) for every 300mm (1ft) of pipe run. It should not exceed 3m (10ft) in length.

Choosing a wash basin

Wall-hung and pedestal basins are made from vitreous china, but basins supported all round by a vanity unit counter-top are also made in pressed steel or plastic. Select the taps at the same time to ensure that the basin of your choice has holes at the required spacing to receive the taps, or no holes at all if the taps are to be wall-mounted.

Make sure the basin has sufficient space on each side or to the rear for soaps, shampoo or other toiletries otherwise you will have to provide a separate shelf or cabinet.

Pedestal basins
Although the hollow pedestal provides some additional support to the basin, its main purpose is to conceal unsightly supply pipes.

Wall-hung basin
Older wall-mounted basins are supported on large, screw-fixed brackets but a modern concealed wall mounting is just as strong and provides a far more attractive fixture.

Check that you can fix securely to the studs of a timber frame wall or hack off the plaster and install a mounting board (▷). (Use the same method to secure an existing basin with loose wall fixings.)

If you want to hide supply pipes, consider some form of panelling.

Corner basin
Hand basins which fit into the corner of a room are popular because supply and wastepipes can be run conveniently through adjacent walls or concealed by boxing them in across the corner.

Recessed basin
A small hand basin can be recessed into a wall of a cloakroom or WC where space is limited.

Counter-top basins
In a large bathroom or bedroom, you can fit a wash basin into a counter-top as part of a built-in vanity unit. The cupboards below provide ample storage for towels and toiletries while hiding the plumbing at the same time.

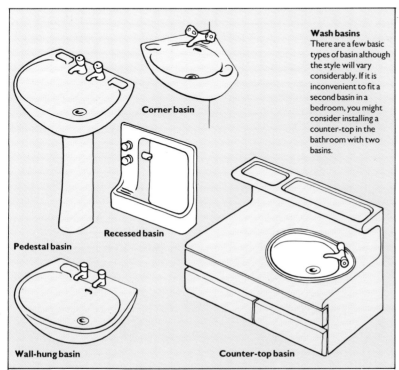

Wash basins
There are a few basic types of basin although the style will vary considerably. If it is inconvenient to fit a second basin in a bedroom, you might consider installing a counter-top in the bathroom with two basins.

Corner basin

Recessed basin

Pedestal basin

Wall-hung basin

Counter-top basin

CONCEALING PIPEWORK

The manufacturers of appliances and fittings are aware that most people find visible plumbing unattractive, and as a result, supply fitments such as sink units, panelled baths, shower cubicles, concealed cisterns, pedestal and counter-top basins, all of which are designed to hide their supply pipes and drainage. With careful selection and intelligently designed pipe runs, it should be possible to plumb your house without a single visible pipe. In practice, however, there are always situations where you have no option but to surface-run at least some pipes, especially when you cannot take them under floorboards. You can minimize the effect by taking special care to group pipes together neatly, and keep runs both straight and parallel. When painted to match the skirtings or walls, such pipes are practically invisible.

Alternatively, you can construct ducting to conceal pipes completely. Make your own ducting with softwood battens and plywood to bridge the corner of a room, or construct a false skirting deep enough to contain the pipes. It is a wise precaution to make at least part of the ducting removable to gain access to joints or other fittings in case you need to service them at a later date. For total accessibility, use proprietary ducting made from PVC. It is manufactured in a range of sizes to contain grouped or individual pipes. With right-angle and tee-piece joints, you can construct a system of ducting to cover any new or existing installation. Optional foam liners insulate hot water or central heating pipes.

Clip pipes into plastic ducting

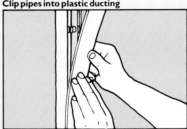

Snap on the matching cover-strips.

Space for a basin
Allow extra elbow room for washing hair. A space 1100mm (3ft 8in) x 700mm (2ft 4in) should be sufficient. To suit most people, position the rim of a basin 800mm (2ft 8in) from the floor.

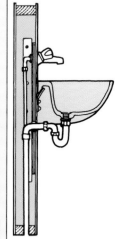

Mounting a basin
Fix a wall-mounted hand basin and taps to an exterior-grade plywood board.

SELECTING TAPS FOR A BASIN

SEE ALSO

◁ Details for:
| Repairing taps | 10-11 |

Most taps are made of chromium plated or enamelled brass although there is a limited range of plastic-bodied taps. Plastic taps are not as durable as metal ones but they are considerably cheaper. All basin taps have a 15mm ($\frac{1}{2}$in) threaded inlet known as the tail for attaching the supply pipe.

Types of tap

Individual taps
The majority of wash basins are fitted with individual taps for the hot and cold water supply. Cross or capstan head taps are still manufactured for traditionally-styled bathrooms but most taps have a metal or plastic shrouded head. A lever head tap turns the tap from off to full on with one quarter turn only. They are especially convenient for the elderly or disabled.

Individual wall-mounted taps are known as bib taps while those fixed directly to the basin itself are called pillar taps.

Shrouded-head tap

Lever-head tap

Mixer taps
A mixer tap has a hot and cold valve linked to a common spout. Water is provided at the required temperature by adjusting the two valves simultaneously.

Basin mixer taps often incorporate a pop-up waste. A series of inter-linking rods, operated by a button on the centre of the mixer, open and close the waste plug in the basin.

Normally, the body of the tap which connects the valves and spout, rests on the upper surface of the basin. The tails only protrude through holes in the basin to meet the supply pipes. This is a two-hole mixer with tails spaced 100mm (4in) apart.

A three-hole mixer appears to have separate valves and spout but they are linked by a tube below the basin. The tube is cut to length to accommodate the distance between the holes in the basin which may be from 200 to 250mm (8 to 10in) apart.

Both inlets of a one-hole mixer pass through the same hole.

An entire mixer set can be mounted on a wall above the basin. Alternatively, the valves can be mounted on the basin yet still divert hot and cold water to a wall-mounted spout.

Two-hole mixer

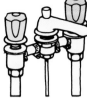

Three-hole mixer

One-hole mixer

TAP MECHANISMS

Over recent years there have been revolutionary changes in tap design, and not just in their appearance or styling. Entirely new thinking about the function of a tap has provided the consumer with taps that are easier to operate, more hard-wearing and simpler to maintain.

Rising-spindle taps
Within a traditionally designed tap, the entire spindle, jumper and washer move up and down, turning along with the head when you operate the tap.

Non-rising head taps
Outwardly, these taps resemble a rising-spindle tap but when the head turns, it does not move up and down. Instead, it causes a threaded spindle and washer unit to rise vertically without turning. Because the washer is not twisted against the seat as the valve is closed, neither the washer nor seat wear as quickly as those in a conventional tap.

Ceramic disc taps
Precision ground ceramic discs replace the traditional washer, but instead of separating, one disc rotates on the other so that waterways through them gradually align with each other allowing water to flow. There is virtually no wear as hard water scale or other debris cannot interfere with the fit of the discs. If a problem develops, the whole mechanism is replaced.

Reverse-pressure taps
An original concept in tap design. The head and spout hang from the water inlet and move as one unit forcing the washer upwards against the seat. A unique check valve inside the tap shuts off the water as the tap is dismantled to change a washer.

Electronic taps
Water flows automatically from an electronic tap as soon as an integral photo-cell detects the presence of your hands under the spout. It stops flowing when you remove your hands. The tap is powered by a transformer mounted beneath the basin or vanity unit. Water temperature is regulated by a control on the body of the tap.

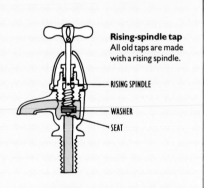

Rising-spindle tap
All old taps are made with a rising spindle.

RISING SPINDLE

WASHER

SEAT

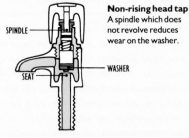

Non-rising head tap
A spindle which does not revolve reduces wear on the washer.

SPINDLE

SEAT

WASHER

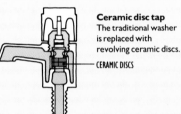

Ceramic disc tap
The traditional washer is replaced with revolving ceramic discs.

CERAMIC DISCS

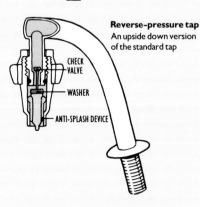

Reverse-pressure tap
An upside down version of the standard tap

CHECK VALVE

WASHER

ANTI-SPLASH DEVICE

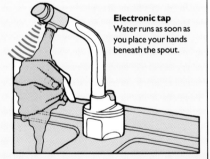

Electronic tap
Water runs as soon as you place your hands beneath the spout.

REPLACING OLD TAPS

When replacing taps, you will want to use the existing plumbing if possible but it can be difficult to disconnect old corroded fittings. Apply penetrating oil to the tap connectors and to the back-nuts clamping the tap to the basin. While the oil takes effect, shut off the cold and hot water supply.

Applying heat with a gas torch can break down corrosion by expanding metal fittings, but wrap a wet cloth around nearby soldered joints or you may melt the solder. Take care that you do not damage a plastic waste and trap, and protect flammable surfaces with a ceramic tile. Too much heat may crack a ceramic basin.

It is not always possible to engage the nuts with a standard wrench. Instead, hire a special cranked spanner designed to reach into the confined spaces below a basin or bath. You can apply extra leverage to the spanner by slipping a stout metal bar or wrench handle into the other end.

Having disconnected the pipework, tap the bottom of the tap tails with a wooden mallet to break the seal of plumbers' putty under the taps. Clean the remnants of putty from around the taps holes and fit new taps. If the tap tails are shorter than the originals, or the threads do not match the tap connectors, check a manufacturer's catalogue for various adaptors.

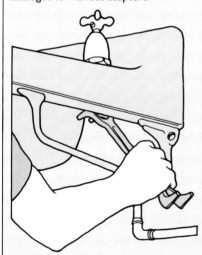

Releasing a tap connector
Use a special cranked spanner to release the fixing nut of a tap connector.

A cranked spanner fits basin and bath taps

FIXING A WALL-HUNG BASIN

Turn off the supply of water to an old basin before you disconnect it (▷). However, you can save some time by fitting the new taps to its replacement beforehand so that you are not without water in the meantime.

Removing the old basin

If you want to use existing plumbing, loosen the compression nuts on the tap tails (see left) and trap, otherwise cut through the waste and supply pipes at a point where you can most easily connect new plumbing (**1**).

Remove any fixings holding the basin to its support brackets or pedestal and lift it from the wall. Apply penetrating oil to the bracket wall fixings in an attempt to remove them without damaging the plaster, but as a last resort, lever the brackets off the wall. Take care not to break cast iron fittings as they can be quite valuable.

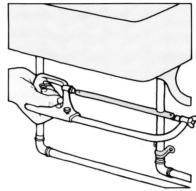

1 Cut through old supply pipes with a hacksaw

Fitting new taps

Fit new taps to the basin before fixing it to the wall. Slip a plastic washer supplied with the tap onto its tail, then pass the tail through the hole in the basin. If no washer is supplied, spread some plumbers' putty around the top of the tail and beneath the base of the tap.

With the basin resting on its rim, slip a second washer onto the tail then hand tighten the back-nut to clamp the tap onto the basin (**2**). Check that the spout faces into the basin then tighten the back-nut carefully with a cranked spanner (See left).

Wipe excess putty from the basin then fit the second tap.

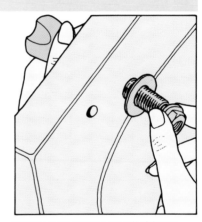

2 Slip the back-nut onto the tail of the tap

Fixing the basin to the wall

Have an assistant hold the basin against the wall at the required height and check it is horizontal with a spirit level, then mark the fixing holes for the wall bracket (**3**). Lay the basin to one side while you drill and plug the fixing holes.

Screw the bracket securely to the wall and bolt the basin to it with whatever fixings are supplied by the manufacturer. Connect the plumbing to the taps and fit the waste system (▷).

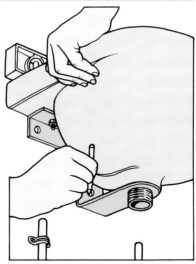

3 Mark the bracket fixing holes on the wall

SEE ALSO	
Details for: ▷	
Turning off water	8
Connecting pipes	20-27
Hacksaws	72-73
Gas torch	74
Spanners and wrenches	75-76

CONNECTING A WALL-HUNG BASIN

Once you have fitted new taps and mounted the basin on the wall (◁), finish the installation by connecting the waste system along with the hot and cold supply pipes.

A pressed-metal basin
When you fit taps to a pressed-metal basin, slip built-up 'top hat' washers onto the tails to cover the shanks. The basin itself may be supplied with a rubber strip to seal the joint with the counter-top. It will need a combined waste and overflow like a bath (◁).

● **Counter-top basin**
Manufacturers supply a template for cutting the hole in a counter-top to receive the basin. Run mastic around the edge to seal a ceramic basin, and clamp it with the fixings supplied.

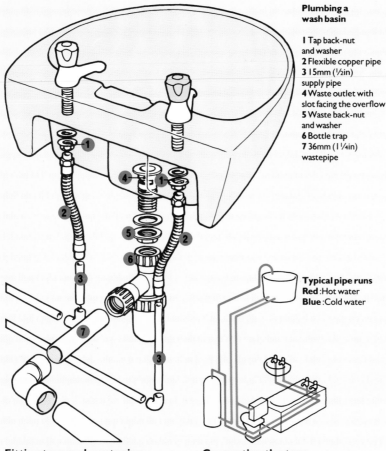

Plumbing a wash basin

1 Tap back-nut and washer
2 Flexible copper pipe
3 15mm (½in) supply pipe
4 Waste outlet with slot facing the overflow
5 Waste back-nut and washer
6 Bottle trap
7 36mm (1¼in) wastepipe

Typical pipe runs
Red: Hot water
Blue: Cold water

Fitting trap and wastepipe

Fit the waste outlet into the bottom of the basin as for taps using washers or plumbers' putty to form a watertight seal. The basin will probably have an integral overflow running to the waste, in which case ensure that the slot in the waste outlet aligns with the overflow. Tighten the back-nut under the basin while holding the outlet still by gripping its grille with pliers.

If you can utilize the existing wastepipe, connect the trap to the waste outlet and to the end of the pipe. A two-part trap provides some adjustment to align it with the old wastepipe.

If necessary, run a new 36mm (1¼in) wastepipe, cutting a hole through the wall with a masonry drill and cold chisel. Run the pipe, with sufficient fall – 6mm (¼in) per 300mm (1ft) run – to terminate over the hopper on top of the vertical wastepipe. Fix the pipe to the wall with saddle clips.

Connecting the taps

You can run standard 15mm (½in) copper or plastic pipes to the taps and join them with tap connectors, but it is easier to use short lengths of flexible, corrugated copper pipe specially designed for tap connection. They can be bent by hand to allow for any slight misalignment between the supply pipes and tap tails. Each corrugated pipe has a tap connector at one end, and at the other, a compression or capillary joint.

Connect the corrugated pipes to the tap tails but leave them hand tight only, then run new branch pipework to meet them. Make soldered or compression joints to connect the pipes (◁). Tighten the tap connectors with a cranked spanner (◁).

Turn on the water supply and check the pipes for leaks. Drain the system to repair a weeping joint (◁).

Connecting waste to soil pipe

Connect a basin wastepipe to a single stack, plastic soil pipe with a proprietary pipe boss. A boss may be connected by other methods, but is often clamped to the soil pipe with a strap.

Mark where the basin waste meets the soil pipe and cut a hole of the recommended diameter with a hole saw (**1**). Smooth the edge of the hole with abrasive paper.

Wipe both contacting surfaces with the manufacturer's cleaner, then apply gap-filling solvent cement around the hole. Strap the boss over the hole and tighten the bolt (**2**).

Insert the rubber lining in the boss in preparation for the wastepipe (**3**).

Lubricate the end of the pipe and push it firmly into the boss (**4**). Clip the pipe to the wall.

1 Cut a hole in the pipe with a hole saw

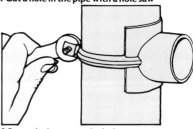

2 Strap the boss over the hole

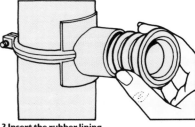

3 Insert the rubber lining

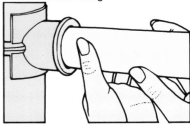

4 Push the wastepipe into the boss

INSTALLING A NEW BATH

There are companies who will re-enamel your old bath – some will even spray it in-situ. If you own an attractive, antique cast iron bath it would be worth asking for quotations before you make up your mind to discard it. Even if you don't want the bath yourself, you may be able to sell it to a company who specializes in bath restoration. On the other hand, most old baths are simply too ugly to restore, and it may prove to be more economical to replace one that is badly chipped or stained. If a bath is cracked, it is beyond repair.

Choosing a bath

You can buy reproduction or even restored Victorian baths in cast iron from specialist suppliers but they are likely to be expensive. In practical terms, a cast iron bath is far too heavy for one person to handle: even two people would have difficulty carrying one to an upstairs bathroom. A cast iron bath can look splendid when left freestanding in a room, but it can be virtually impossible to clean behind one, and panelling-in the curved and sometimes tapering shape is rarely successful.

Nowadays, the majority of baths are made from enamelled pressed steel, acrylic or glass-reinforced plastic. Two people can handle a steel bath with ease and you could carry a plastic bath on your own. Although modern plastic baths are strong and durable, some are harmed by abrasive cleaners, bleach and especially heat. It is not advisable to use a gas torch near a plastic bath.

When it comes to style and colour, there is no lack of choice in any material, although the more unconventional baths are likely to be made of plastic. Nearly every bath comes with matching panels and optional features like hand grips and dropped sides to make it easier to step in and out. Taps do not have to be mounted at the foot of the bath. Many manufacturers offer alternative corner or side mounting facilities. Some will even cut tap holes to order.

You can order a bath in any style to double as a jacuzzi, but the plumbing is somewhat complicated so you will need to have it professionally installed.

Rectangular bath

A standard, rectangular bath is still the most popular and economical design. Baths vary in size from 1.5 to 1.8m (5 to 6ft) in length, with a choice of widths from 700 to 800mm (2ft 4in to 2ft 8in)

Corner bath

A corner bath occupies more actual floor area than a rectangular bath of the same capacity, but because the tub itself is turned at an angle to the room, it may take up less wall-space. A corner bath always provides generous shelf space for essential toiletries.

Round bath

A round bath would prove to be impractical in most bathrooms, but if you are converting a spare bedroom, you may decide to make the bath a feature of interior design as well as a practical appliance.

Selecting taps for a bath

The basic design and style of bath taps are identical to basin taps (▷), but they are proportionally larger with 22mm (¾in) tails. Individual hot and cold taps or mixers are made to fit a bath with hole centres 180mm (7⅛in) apart.

Some bath mixers are designed to supply water to a shower head, either mounted telephone-style on the mixer itself, or hung from a bracket mounted on a wall above the bath (▷).

SUPPORTING A PLASTIC BATH

A metal frame is supplied to cradle a flexible plastic bath. Without it, the bath would distort and possibly crack.

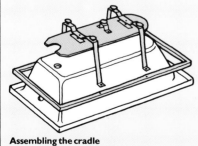

Assembling the cradle
Turn a bath on its rim to fit the cradle.

TYPES OF BATH

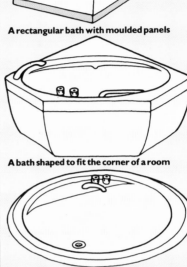

A rectangular bath with moulded panels

A bath shaped to fit the corner of a room

A circular bath fits flush with the floor

RENOVATING BATH ENAMEL

You can buy two-part paints prepared specifically to restore the enamel surface of an old bath, sink or basin. To achieve a first-class result, the bath must be scrupulously clean and dry, so tape plastic bags over the taps to prevent water dripping into the bath and work in a warm atmosphere where condensation will not occur. Wipe the surface with a cloth dampened with white spirit to remove traces of grease, then paint the bath from the bottom upwards in a circular direction. This type of paint is self-levelling so don't brush it out too much. Pick up runs or tears immediately and work fairly quickly to keep the wet edge fresh.

For a professional finish, hire a company which will send an operator to spray a stained bath in-situ. The whole process should take no longer than two to three hours. The bath is cleaned chemically before a grinder is used to key the surface and remove heavy stains. Chipped enamel can be repaired at the same time. Finally, surrounding areas are masked before the bath is sprayed.

SEE ALSO

Details for: ▷	
Selecting taps	32
Shower mixer	38
Plumbing a bath	36
Panelling a bath	37

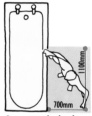

Access to the bath
Allow a space of 1100 x 700mm (3ft 8in x 2ft 4in) beside the bath to climb in and out safely, and for bathing younger members of the family.

PLUMBING THE BATH

Waste/overflow units
A flexible tube takes overflow water to the trap.

Compression unit
Runs to cleaning eye on the trap.

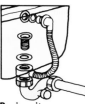

Banjo unit
Slips over tail of waste outlet.

WC and bath overflow
Overflow from a WC joins the bath unit.

Shallow-seal trap
Use this type of trap when space is limited but it must discharge to a yard gully.

Once a bath is fitted close to the walls of a bathroom, it can be difficult to make the joints and connections, so fit the taps, overflow and trap before you push the new bath into position and prior to removing the existing bath.

Fit adjustable feet to the new bath or suspend a plastic bath in its supporting cradle according to the manufacturer's instructions.

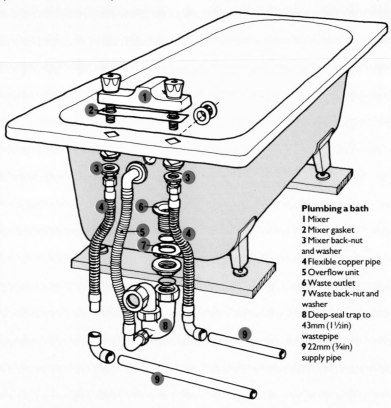

Plumbing a bath
1 Mixer
2 Mixer gasket
3 Mixer back-nut and washer
4 Flexible copper pipe
5 Overflow unit
6 Waste outlet
7 Waste back-nut and washer
8 Deep-seal trap to 43mm (1½in) wastepipe
9 22mm (¾in) supply pipe

Fitting the taps
Fit individual hot and cold taps as for a wash basin (◁). Fitting a mixer is a similar procedure, but most units are supplied with a long sealing gasket which slips over both tails. Drop the tails through the holes in the rim, slip top-hat washers onto them (◁) and tighten both back-nuts to clamp the mixer to the bath.

Fit a flexible 22mm (¾in) copper pipe (similar to those used for washbasin taps) onto each tail. As an alternative, you can attach short lengths of standard 22mm (¾in) copper or plastic pipe with tap connectors in preparation for jointing to the pipe run, but the flexible pipes allow for adjustment in case joints are slightly misaligned.

Fitting waste and overflow
Fit a combined waste and overflow unit. A flexible plastic hose takes water from the overflow outlet in the end of the bath to the waste outlet or trap. If you use a 'banjo' unit, you must fit the overflow before the trap, but the flexible pipe of a compression fitting unit connects to the trap itself. (See left)

Spread a layer of plumbers' putty under the rim of the waste outlet, or fit a circular rubber seal. Before inserting its tail into the hole in the bottom of the bath, seal the thread with PTFE tape. On the underside, add a plastic washer then tighten the large back-nut, bedding the outlet down onto the putty or rubber seal. Wipe off excess putty before it sets.

Connect the bath trap (see left) to the tail of the waste outlet with its own compression nut. (Fit a banjo overflow unit at the same time.)

Pass the threaded boss of the overflow hose through the hole in the end of the bath. Slip a washer seal over the boss, then use a pair of pliers to screw on the overflow outlet grille.

If you are using a compression fitting overflow, connect the nut on the other end of the hose to the cleaning eye of the trap.

Removing the old bath
Turn off the hot and cold water supply, then drain the system (◁).

Have a shallow bowl ready to catch any trapped water, then use a junior hacksaw to cut through the old supply and wastepipes. As the overflow from an old bath will almost certainly exit through the wall, saw through it at the same time.

If adjustable feet are fitted to the bath, lower them, pushing down on the bath to break the mastic seal between the rim and bathroom walls. Pull the bath away from the wall.

If you don't want to preserve a cast iron bath, it will be easier to break it up in the bathroom and carry it out in pieces. Wear protective goggles and ear protectors, drape a dust sheet over the bath then smash it with a heavy hammer.

Hack the old overflow from the wall with a cold chisel, fill the hole with mortar, and repair the plasterwork.

Installing the new bath
Run new 22mm (¾in) supply pipes, or attach spurs to the existing ones, ready for connection to the flexible pipes already fitted on the bath taps.

Cut two boards to support the feet of the bath and spread the point load over a wider area. Slide the bath into position and adjust the height of the feet with a spanner. Use a spirit level to check that the rim is horizontal.

Adjust the flexible tap pipes and join them to the supply pipes (◁).

Connect a 43mm (1½in) wastepipe to the trap and run it to the external hopper or soil stack as for a wash basin (◁). Restore the water supply and check for leaks before you fix the bath panels.

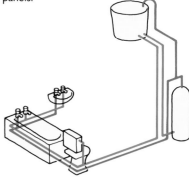

Typical bathroom pipe runs
Red: Hot water – **Blue**: Cold water.

Panelling a bath

In all probability, your bath will be supplied with moulded polystyrene panels to hide the plumbing and facilitate cleaning.

You can panel a basic rectangular bath with a softwood framework supporting a sheet of hardboard or plywood. The finish is a matter of personal choice. You can paint a standard plain hardboard or apply a wall covering to match or contrast with the bathroom decor. Alternatively, use a melamine-faced board – a practical, easy-to-clean surface – or add a texture with an embossed hardboard. You could continue the floorcovering up the panel using an adhesive to attach carpet, vinyl or cork tiles. If you want to use ceramic tiles, provide a small removable panel at the end of the bath so that you can service the plumbing. Design the panel to break between two rows of tiles.

When a bath does not fit against a wall at both ends, either continue the panelling around the exposed end, or make a fixed shelf of tiled marine plywood to fit behind the head or taps, and run the panelling from wall to wall.

Make the framework of 50mm x 25mm (2in x 1in) sawn softwood. Simple butt joints held together with timber connectors will suffice as the fixed sheet will make the frame rigid.

Scribe the sheet to fit under the rim of the bath and to fit the wall at each end, then pin and glue it to the framework. If pinning would spoil the surface, use planed timber for the frame and attach the sheet with adhesive.

Screw a vertical batten to the wall at each end of the bath to support the panelled frame and nail one or two softwood blocks to the floor for the frame to rest against. Screw the finished panel to the battens with brass screws and screw caps. Alternatively, use magnetic catches and fit small knobs or handles to the panel.

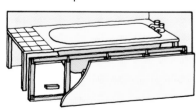

Panelling a bath
This example shows wall-to-wall panelling with a tiled shelf to fill the gap, but you can use a similar construction to fit any situation.

CHOOSING A SHOWER

Soaking in a bath tub is very relaxing but taking a shower is more invigorating and hygienic while using far less hot water. A shower cubicle occupies a 750mm (2ft 6in) square of floor space so it is quite possible to locate one somewhere other than the bathroom. The corner of a bedroom is an obvious choice but you may prefer to convert a downstairs cloakroom or install a shower in a utility room along with the washing machine and tumble dryer. A separate shower can be a boon to a busy family who would otherwise queue for a single bathroom before leaving for work or school.

IMPORTANT CONSIDERATIONS

A shower must comply with certain requirements to satisfy the water authority and provide you with a facility which is both safe and comfortable.

Equal water pressure

The hot and cold water supply to a shower must be under equal pressure. You must never mix hot water from a cylinder with mains pressure cold water. The cold water must be supplied from the storage cistern. It is against water authority regulations to mix mains and stored water and, in any case, it would be difficult to maintain a comfortable temperature at the shower.

Sufficient pressure

Unless the water pressure is high enough, the performance of your shower will never be satisfactory. Apart from a mains pressure instantaneous shower, water pressure is determined by the height of the cold water storage cistern. The bottom of the cistern should be 1.5m (5ft) or more above the shower head. A shower can work satisfactorily when the shower head is only 900mm (3ft) below the cistern but only if the pipe run is short and straight.

Hot water pressure is unaffected by the position of the cylinder as it is supplied initially from the same cold water cistern and therefore its pressure is equal to the cold water supply.

When the pressure is insufficient, you can either raise the cistern on a strong wooden frame which means lengthening all the existing pipes, or you can fit a pump to boost the shower pressure.

Independent supply

If your shower is fed by branch pipes connected to the rest of the bathroom plumbing, there is a risk that water pressure will drop if someone draws water at another appliance. If it is the pressure on the hot supply that drops, then your shower will suddenly run cold which is merely unpleasant, but if pressure drops on the cold supply, the shower could become dangerously hot.

Ideally, the cold supply should be a 15mm (½in) pipe run independently from the storage cistern, and the hot supply should be a 15mm (½in) branch pipe taken directly from the vent pipe above the cylinder. Independent pipe runs are not essential if you install a thermostatic shower which can cope with slight variations in pressure.

Drainage

Because a shower tray stands on the floor, it can be difficult to obtain the minimum fall of 6mm (¼in) per 300mm (1ft) run of wastepipe. You may be able to run the waste under floorboards, but only if the joists run in the same direction as the pipe. Sometimes it is necessary to raise the tray on a plinth.

SHOWER UNITS

Installing an independent shower cubicle with its own supply and waste system requires some previous experience of plumbing but if you utilize an existing bath as a shower tray, fitting a shower unit can involve little more than replacing the taps.

Bath/shower mixer

This type of shower is the simplest to install. It is connected like a standard bath mixer to the existing 22mm (¾in) cold and hot water pipes, while the bath waste system takes care of the drainage. Having obtained the required temperature at the spout by adjusting the hot and cold valves, lifting a button on the mixer diverts the water, via a flexible hose, to the shower head. The shower head can be hand-held for washing hair, or hung from a wall-mounted bracket to provide a conventional shower.

You must not fit a bath/shower mixer when cold water is supplied under mains pressure to the bath tap. As the supply pipes are already part of the bathroom plumbing network, it is impossible to guard against fluctuating pressure unless the mixer is fitted with a thermostatic valve. If the pressure is insufficient, fit a booster pump.

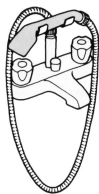

Bath/shower mixer
Fit this type of shower unit like an ordinary bath mixer.

Thermostatic shower mixer

A thermostatic mixer is similar in design to a manual version but another control is incorporated to pre-set the water temperature. If the pressure drops on either the hot or cold supply, the thermostatic valve compensates by lowering the pressure on the other side. Consequently, you can supply a thermostatic shower with branch pipes from the bathroom plumbing but try to join them as near as possible to the cold cistern and hot cylinder.

The mixer cannot raise the pressure of the supply: you still need a booster pump if it is low. Neither will it compensate for the considerable difference in pressure between mains and gravity fed water.

Thermostatic mixer
This unit has separate controls for flow and temperature.

Manual shower mixer (near right)
A unit with a single control to regulate the rate of flow and the temperature of the water.

Booster pump (far right)
The simplest type of pump is mounted to the shower wall between the mixer and shower head.

Manual shower mixer

A manual shower mixer can be mounted on the wall above a bathtub, but with its own supply of hot and cold water, or it can be situated in a separate shower cubicle. Simple mixers have individual hot and cold valves, but most manual shower mixers have a single control which regulates flow and water temperature. A manual mixer must have independent hot and cold supply.

Booster pump

If your existing shower installation is unsatisfactory due to low pressure, you can improve its performance by adding an electric booster pump. Some pumps are designed for remote installation, usually in an airing cupboard next to the hot water cylinder. Hot and cold pipes are fed to the pump, then out again to the shower mixer.

So long as you don't object to it being visible, it is simpler to mount a pump in the shower cubicle or over the bath. No extra plumbing is required as the pump is connected to the shower mixer by a flexible metal hose. A two core and earth electrical cable runs from the pump to a switched, fused connection unit (◁) which must be clearly identified and accessible, but out of reach of anyone using the shower or bath.

If you want to install a new shower where water pressure is low, buy a shower unit with an integral pump.

Manual shower mixer   **Booster pump**

INSTANTANEOUS SHOWER

An instantaneous shower solves many problems associated with other types of shower. It is designed specifically for connection to the mains water supply with one 15mm (½in) branch pipe from the rising main. Because the rising main passes through every floor of the house, you can install an instantaneous shower practically anywhere so long as drainage is feasible. Incoming water is heated within the unit so there is no separate hot water supply to balance. The shower is thermostatically controlled to prevent fluctuations in pressure affecting the water temperature – in fact it switches off completely if there is a serious failure of pressure.

Most instantaneous showers are electrically powered and require their own 30amp circuit from the consumer unit. A ceiling-mounted, 30 amp, double pole switch must be connected to the circuit to turn the appliance on and off (◁). Gas-heated showers are available but they should be installed by a qualified fitter.

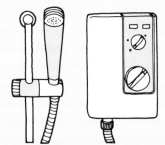

An instantaneous shower control unit
A detachable shower head is connected to the control unit by a flexible hose.

ELECTRICAL INSTALLATIONS

Electrical installations in a bathroom are dangerous unless they conform to the current Institute of Electrical Engineers wiring regulations. Read the electrical section in this book and manufacturers' instructions carefully to make sure you understand thoroughly the requirements for wiring in a bathroom before undertaking the work. If you are in any doubt, or have had no previous experience, hire a qualified electrician.

CONSTRUCTING A SHOWER CUBICLE

Without doubt, the simplest way to acquire a shower cubicle is to install a factory-assembled cabinet, complete with tray and shower mixer, together with waterproof doors or a curtain to contain the spray from the shower head. Having run supply pipes and drainage, the installation is complete. However, the cabinets are expensive. The alternative is to construct a purpose-made shower cubicle to fit exactly the space you have allocated.

SHOWER TRAYS

Shower trays are made from enamelled cast iron or steel, ceramics or glass-reinforced plastic. Metal or ceramic trays are substantial but heavy, and may require two people to move them into position. Plastic trays are lightweight and cheap but they have a tendency to flex slightly in use so it is particularly important to seal the edges carefully with a flexible mastic instead of relying on grout. Whatever material you choose, you should have no problem finding a colour to match other bathroom appliances.

Trays are between 750mm (2ft 6in) and 900mm (3ft) square. Most are designed to stand on the floor with a surrounding apron about 150mm (6in) in height. Some have adjustable feet to level the tray, or even a metal underframe to raise it off the floor to provide a fall for the waste-pipe. A plinth screwed across the front of the tray hides the underframe and plumbing while providing access to the trap for servicing. Some trays are intended to be flush with the floor.

A round waste outlet fits in the bottom of the tray much like a bath but it is not slotted to accommodate an overflow. Fit a space-saving, shallow-seal trap to the outlet.

Floor-standing tray

Recessed tray

Choosing the site

When you are deciding upon the location of your shower, consider how you are going to build the walls of the cubicle. Some sites will involve more work than others.

Free-standing
You can place the shower tray against a flat wall and either construct a stud partition (▷) on each side, or surround the tray with a proprietary shower enclosure.

Corner site
If you place the tray in a corner of a room, two sides of the cubicle are ready-made. Either run a curtain around the tray or install a corner-entry enclosure with sliding doors. Alternatively, build a fixed side wall yourself and place a door or curtain across the entrance.

Built-in cupboards
Blend a shower cubicle into a bedroom by placing it into a corner as described above, then construct a built-in wardrobe unit between the shower and the opposite wall.

Concealing the plumbing

A shower with exposed pipework will work perfectly well but it spoils the appearance of the cubicle. You could install a proprietary rigid plastic pillar in the corner of the cubicle to cover the pipework and house the mixer and shower head.

If you erect a stud partition (▷) on one side, you can run the plumbing between the studs. Screw and glue exterior-grade plywood on the inside of the frame as a mounting board for the shower mixer and spray head. Connect the plumbing to the mixer before you panel the outside of the framework.

Cover the plywood panel with ceramic tiles or, alternatively, use a melamine-faced board, attaching it to the framework with metal angle-brackets. Prime the edges of the board and apply a mastic seal where it meets the wall and tray.

Running plumbing through a partition ▷
Conceal pipework in a simple timber partition covered with plywood and ceramic tiles.

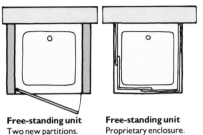

Free-standing unit
Two new partitions.

Free-standing unit
Proprietary enclosure.

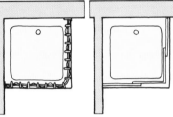

Corner site
Enclosed by a curtain.

Corner site
Proprietary enclosure.

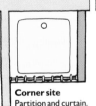

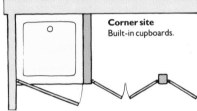

Corner site
Built-in cupboards.

Corner site
Partition and curtain.

SEE ALSO

Details for: ▷
Stud partition   77

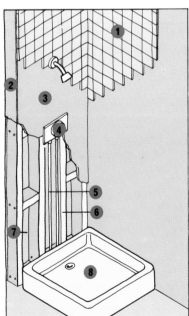

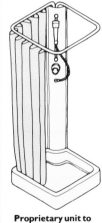

Proprietary unit to conceal plumbing
The plastic corner pillar, shower set, tray and curtain are designed as a complete system.

1 Ceramic tiles
2 Timber cover strip
3 Exterior-grade plywood
4 Shower mixer
5 Pipework
6 Timber frame
7 Plasterboard
8 Shower tray

PROCEDURE FOR INSTALLING A SHOWER

Use the procedure below as a guide to the stage by stage installation of a shower and cubicle. Follow the instructions on fitting plastic or copper supply pipes and drainage (◁), and take note of the manufacturer's recommendations for the particular shower unit you are installing.

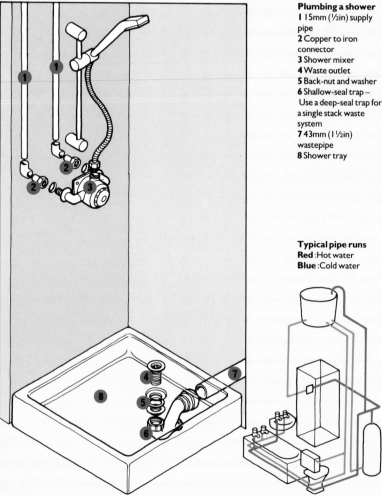

Plumbing a shower
1 15mm (½in) supply pipe
2 Copper to iron connector
3 Shower mixer
4 Waste outlet
5 Back-nut and washer
6 Shallow-seal trap – Use a deep-seal trap for a single stack waste system
7 43mm (1½in) wastepipe
8 Shower tray

Typical pipe runs
Red : Hot water
Blue : Cold water

● Fit the waste outlet in the shower tray and connect a shallow-seal trap as for a bath (◁).

● Install the tray and run a 43mm (1½in) wastepipe to the outside hopper. To connect it to a waste stack with a strap boss (◁), use a deep-seal trap.

● To enclose a shower, construct a stud partition on one side and line the inner surface with exterior-grade plywood.

● Cut a hole in the board for a flush-mounted shower mixer, or drill holes for the supply pipes to a surface-mounted version.

● Assemble the shower mixer and head according to the manufacturer's instructions.

● Connect it to 15mm (½in) pipes, running them back to the supply (◁). Turn off the water and join the pipes to the supply. Turn the water on again then test the installation for leaks (◁).

● Panel or plasterboard the outside of the stud partition and tile the inside of the cubicle using waterproof adhesive and grout (◁).

● Erect the shower enclosure or fit a shower rail and curtain.

● Seal around the edges of the tray with a flexible mastic.

Instantaneous showers

If you want to install an instanteous shower in the cubicle, run the electrical supply cable, and a single 15mm (½in) pipe from the rising main, through the stud partition (◁). Drill two holes in the wall behind the shower unit for the pipe and cable. Join a threaded or compression connector to the supply pipe, whichever is appropriate for the water inlet built into the shower unit. Make the electrical connections to the shower as recommended by the manufacturer and read the instructions for wiring a shower (◁).

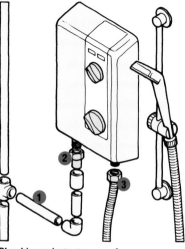

Plumbing an instantaneous shower
1 15mm (½in) pipe from rising main
2 Tap connector
3 Hose to shower head

Enclosing the shower

Showers in cubicles and over bath tubs must be provided with some means of preventing water spraying out onto the floor. Hanging a plastic curtain across the entrance is the simplest and cheapest method. Fit a ceiling-mounted curtain track or a tubular shower rail.

Even when a curtain is tucked into the shower tray, water always seems to escape around the sides of the curtain, or at least drips onto the floor when it is drawn aside. Make a more satisfactory enclosure with metal-framed glass or plastic panels. Hinged, sliding or concertina doors operate within an adjustable frame fixed to the top edge of the tray and the side walls. Bed the lower track onto mastic to make a waterproof joint with the tray and, having completed the enclosure, run a bead of mastic between the framework and the tiled walls of the cubicle.

PLUMBING A BIDET

Although a bidet is primarily for washing the lower parts of the body and genitals, it can double as a footbath for the elderly and small children. Due to the stringent requirements of the water authority, installing a bidet can be an expensive and time consuming procedure. However, if you opt for the simpler version, it is just like plumbing a wash basin.

Over-rim supply bidet

This type of bidet is simply a low level basin. It is fitted with individual hot and cold taps or a basin mixer, and has a built-in overflow running to the waste outlet in the basin. There's only one disadvantage with an over-rim bidet: it is cold when you sit astride it.

Rim supply bidet

A more sophisticated bidet delivers warm water to the basin via a hollow rim. Consequently the rim is pre-heated and comfortable to sit on. A special mixer set with a douche spray is fitted to this type of bidet. It incorporates the normal hot and cold valves but a control in the centre of the mixer diverts water from the rim to the spray head mounted in the bottom of the basin. Because the spray head is submerged when the basin is full, water authority regulations stipulate that a rim supply bidet must take its cold water directly from the storage cistern and there must be no other connections to that pipe. Similarly, the hot water supply must be completely independent and connected to the vent pipe immediately above the cylinder. Check with your water authority before you install a bidet to make sure you comply with local regulations.

INSTALLING A BIDET

When plumbing an over-rim supply bidet, use exactly the same procedures, pipes and connectors described for plumbing a washbasin (▷). Fit the taps, waste outlet and trap, then use a spirit level to position the bidet before fixing it to the floor with non-corrosive screws and washers. Supply the taps with branch pipes from the existing bathroom plumbing and take the wastepipe to the hopper or stack.

Attach the bidet set and trap to a rim supply appliance following the manufacturer's instructions. Screw the bidet to the floor before running 15mm (½in) supply pipes and a 36mm (1¼in) waste according to the water authority regulations (see left). Connect the cold supply to the cistern at the same level as the existing supply pipe (▷).

Plumbing an over-rim supply bidet
1 Tap
2 Tap back-nut and washer
3 Tap connector
4 15mm (½in) supply pipe
5 Waste outlet
6 Waste back-nut and washer
7 Trap
8 36mm (1¼in) wastepipe

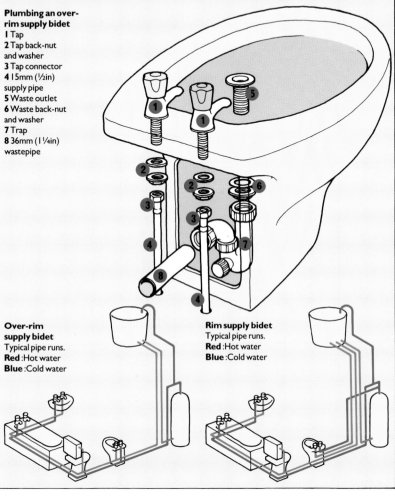

Over-rim supply bidet
Typical pipe runs.
Red: Hot water
Blue: Cold water

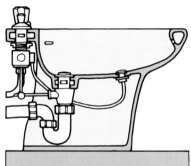

Rim supply bidet
Typical pipe runs.
Red: Hot water
Blue: Cold water

700mm

Space for a bidet
When planning the position of a bidet, allow enough knee room on each side – about 700mm (2ft 3in) overall

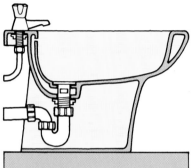

Over-rim supply bidet
This type of bidet is simple to install, just like any wash basin.

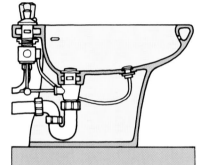

Rim supply bidet
The installation of this type of bidet is complicated by the submerged douche spray. Independent plumbing is essential, and you will need a special mixer set.

FITTING A NEW SINK

A house that has not been improved substantially for perhaps fifty years or more may well have an old fashioned, glazed stoneware sink in the kitchen. Even if you wanted to, it is virtually impossible to incorporate this type of sink into a modern range of kitchen fitments. As it happens, most stoneware sinks were replaced years ago by a stainless steel sinktop incorporating a bowl and drainer in a single pressing, but that too might look somewhat outdated when compared with the present-day colourful alternatives.

SEE ALSO

◁ Details for:
Taps   32

Choosing a kitchen sink

Choose the sink to make the best use of available space, to suit the style of the kitchen, and according to how many other appliances you plan to install which will relieve the sink area of certain functions. Unless your kitchen is fitted with an automatic dishwasher, for instance, the sink must be large enough to cope with a considerable volume of washing-up, and not just the obvious dishes. Don't forget to allow for larger items like baking trays, oven racks and freezer baskets. In addition, check that the bowl is deep enough to fill a bucket from the kitchen tap. If space allows, select a unit with two bowls, primarily for washing and rinsing dishes but also to ensure that one bowl is always free for washing vegetables and salads even when the second is occupied by soaking laundry. If you plan to install a waste disposal unit, one of the bowls must have a waste outlet of the appropriate size (See opposite), or choose a sink unit with a small bowl reserved especially for waste disposal. A double drainer is another useful feature, but if space is limited, allow at least some space to the side of the bowl to avoid piling soiled and clean crockery on a single drainer.

One-piece sinktops are made to modular sizes to fit standard kitchen base units, but sinks which are designed to be set into a continuous work surface offer greater flexibility in size, shape and above all, positioning. What's more, you can set individual bowls or drainers into the worktop to design the layout to suit yourself, and even add a second bowl at a later stage if the need arises. If you opt for this type of installation, choose a drainer equipped with its own waste outlet to drain surface water into the trap beneath the bowl.

Stainless and enamelled steel are still the most popular materials for sinktops, but inset sinks in particular are also made from plastics and ceramic.

Kitchen taps

Kitchen taps are similar in style to those used for wash basins (◁), and there is a kitchen version incorporating the various types of mechanism, but a kitchen mixer has an additional feature. Cold drinking water is supplied from the rising main whereas the hot water at a sink comes from the same storage cylinder that supplies all the other hot taps in the house. As it is against water authority regulations to mix mains and stored water within a fitting, a sink mixer has separate waterways to isolate one supply from the other until the water emerges from the spout. If you are fitting a double-bowl sink, choose a mixer with a swivelling spout. Some sink mixers have an additional hot rinse attachment with a lever-operated spray and detachable brush head for removing stubborn food scraps from crockery and saucepans. Alternatively, you can install an individual attachment supplied by a flexible hose plumbed into the hot water supply pipe below the sink. Make sure the sink you choose is supplied with a hole in the rim to accept the attachment holder.

Individual kitchen taps resemble basin taps in every respect except for their extended pillars to make it possible to fill a bucket in the sink. Sink taps and mixers are provided with 15mm (½in) tails for connecting to the pipes.

Accessories for a kitchen sink

There is a range of accessories designed to fit most kitchen sinks, typically a hardwood or laminated plastic chopping board which drops into the rim of the bowl or drainer, and a selection of plastic-dipped wire baskets for rinsing vegetables or draining crockery and cutlery. Pump-action dispensers for soap and washing-up liquid rid the sink of unsightly plastic bottles and soap dishes.

SINK UNITS, TAPS AND ACCESSORIES

There is a wide variety of kitchen sinks, taps and accessories for the domestic market. Steel, enamel, plastic, double, single, plain and coloured: a bewildering choice when planning your kitchen. Shown below is a cross section of popular sinks, accessories and taps to assist you with your decision.

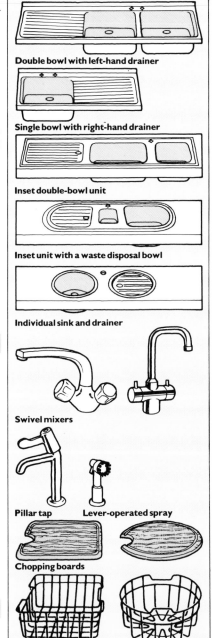

Double bowl with left-hand drainer

Single bowl with right-hand drainer

Inset double-bowl unit

Inset unit with a waste disposal bowl

Individual sink and drainer

Swivel mixers

Pillar tap   **Lever-operated spray**

Chopping boards

Wire baskets

INSTALLING A SINK

The installation of a kitchen sink is essentially the same as fitting a wash basin or vanity unit (▷). All except a ceramic sink will require a combined overflow/waste outlet like a bath (▷). Fit a tubular trap to a sink because a bottle trap blocks too easily.

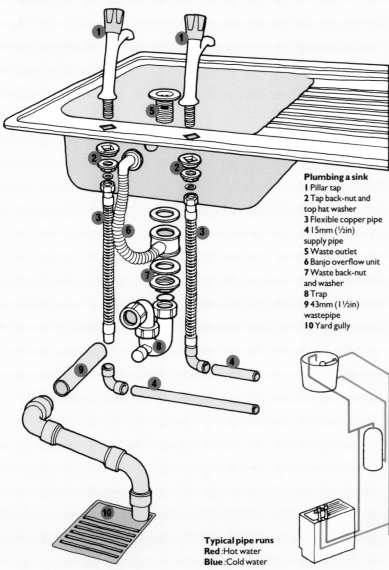

Plumbing a sink
1 Pillar tap
2 Tap back-nut and top hat washer
3 Flexible copper pipe
4 15mm (½in) supply pipe
5 Waste outlet
6 Banjo overflow unit
7 Waste back-nut and washer
8 Trap
9 43mm (1½in) wastepipe
10 Yard gully

Typical pipe runs
Red : Hot water
Blue : Cold water

• Fit the taps, overflow and waste outlet to the sink before you place it in position.

• Turn off the hot and cold supply then remove the old sink by dismantling the plumbing. Hack the old pipes from the wall unless you plan to adapt them.

• Clamp the new sink to its base unit or worktop with the fittings provided, then run a 15mm (½in) cold supply from the rising main and a branch pipe of the same size from the nearest hot water pipe. Connect the pipes to the taps with flexible copper tap conectors (▷). If you prefer to use standard pipe and tap connectors, attach short spur pipes to each tap tail before you install the sink.

• Fit the trap and run a 43mm (1½in) wastepipe through the wall behind the base unit to the yard gully. According to current regulations, the pipe should pass through the grid covering the gully but stop short of the water in the gully trap. Adapt an existing grid by cutting out one corner with a hacksaw.

WASTE DISPOSAL

Waste disposal units

A waste disposal unit provides an hygienic method of dealing with soft food scraps, reserving the kitchen wastebin for dry refuse and bones. The unit houses an electric motor which drives steel cutters for grinding food scraps into a fine slurry which is washed into the yard gully or soil stack. A continuous-feed disposal unit is operated by a manual switch, then, with the cold tap running, scraps are fed into it. To prevent the unit being switched on accidentally, a batch-feed model cannot be operated until a removable plug is inserted in the sink waste outlet.

Most disposal units are designed to fit an 89mm (3½in) outlet in the base of the sink bowl. A special cutter can be hired to adapt a standard stainless steel or plastic sink.

With a sink waste outlet and seal in position (▷), clamp a retaining collar to the outlet from under the sink. Bolt or clip the unit housing to the collar: every unit is supplied with individual instructions.

The waste outlet from the unit itself fits a standard sink trap (not a bottle trap) and wastepipe. If the wastepipe runs to a yard gully, make sure it passes through the covering grid (see left). Wire the unit to a switched, fused connection unit (▷) mounted above the worktop where it is out of the reach of children. Identify the switch to avoid accidental operation.

SEE ALSO	
Details for: ▷	
Fused connection unit	70
Wash basin	33-34
Tap connectors	34
Fitting sink waste	34
Overflow/waste	36
Earthing	68
Connecting pipes	20-27

Cutting a hole for a waste disposal unit
The supplier of the waste disposal unit, or possibly a tool hire company, will rent you a special cutter to convert an existing sink. The cutter cannot be used on a ceramic sink.

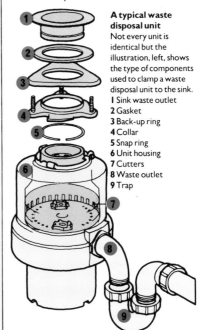

A typical waste disposal unit
Not every unit is identical but the illustration, left, shows the type of components used to clamp a waste disposal unit to the sink.
1 Sink waste outlet
2 Gasket
3 Back-up ring
4 Collar
5 Snap ring
6 Unit housing
7 Cutters
8 Waste outlet
9 Trap

WASHING MACHINES

Appliance valves
Typical valves used to connect washing machines or dishwashers to the water supply.

In-line valve

Right-angle valve

Tee-piece valve

PLUMBING A DISHWASHER AND WASHING MACHINE

The full potential of a dishwasher or washing machine as a labour-saving appliance is somewhat limited if you have to pull it out from under a worksurface before attaching flexible hoses to the kitchen sink. If at all possible, provide any automatic machine with permanent supply and waste systems. Dishwashers need a cold supply only whereas washing machines may be hot and cold fill. Washing machines supplied with hot water provide a faster washing cycle and may be more economical to run depending on how you heat your water. Any retailer will be happy to advise you.

Instructions supplied with the machine should state what water pressure is required. If the machine is installed upstairs, make sure the storage cistern is high enough to provide the required pressure (◁). In a downstairs kitchen or utility room, there is rarely a problem with pressure, especially if you can take the cold water from the mains supply at the sink. However, check with your water authority if you want to connect more than one machine.

Plumbing a washing machine
1 15mm (½in) supply pipe
2 Appliance valve
3 PVC inlet hose
4 Machine inlets
5 Outlet hose
6 Standpipe
7 Trap
8 43mm (1½in) wastepipe to gully

Running the supply

Washing machines and dishwashers are supplied with PVC hoses to link the water inlets at the back of each appliance to special miniature valves connected to the household plumbing. Using these valves, you can turn off the water to service a machine without disrupting the supply to the rest of the house. There are a number of valves to choose from. Select the type which provides the most practical method of connecting to the plumbing depending on the location of the machine in relation to existing pipework.

Self-bore valves

When 15mm (½in) cold and hot water pipes run conveniently behind or alongside the machine, use a valve which bores a hole in the pipe without having to turn off the water supply and drain the system. Each valve is colour coded for hot or cold, and has a threaded outlet for the standard machine hose. Self-bore valves are not approved by all water authorities because the small disc of metal they cut from the pipe may restrict the flow of water. In practice, this hardly ever happens.

To fit a valve, screw the backplate to the wall behind the pipe. Place the saddle with its rubber seal over the pipe. Ensure that the holes in the seal and saddle are aligned before screwing the saddle to the backplate (**1**).

Make sure the valve is turned off then screw it to the saddle (**2**). As you insert the valve, the integral cutter bores a hole in the pipe. With the valve in the vertical position, tighten the adjusting nut with a spanner (**3**). Connect the hose to the valve outlet (**4**).

1 Fit the saddle **2 Insert the valve**

3 Tighten the nut **4 Attach the hose**

Running branch pipes

If you have to extend the plumbing to reach the machine, take branch pipes from the hot and cold pipes supplying the kitchen taps. Terminate the pipes at a convenient position close to the machine and fit a small appliance valve (See left) with a standard compression joint (◁) for connecting to the pipework and a threaded outlet for the hose. When you are fitting this type of valve, turn off the water and drain the system in the normal way (◁). When the supply is restored, open the valve by turning the control level to align with the outlet.

Washing machines and dishwashers are supplied with an outlet hose which must be connected to a waste system to discharge dirty water into a yard gully or single waste stack.

Standpipe and trap

The standard method, approved by all water authorities, employs a vertical 43mm (1½in) plastic standpipe attached to a deep-seal trap. Most plumbing suppliers stock the standpipe, trap and wall fixings as a kit. The machine hose fits loosely in the open-ended pipe to avoid the possibility of dirty water being siphoned back into the machine. Check with the machine manufacturer's instructions regarding the position of the standpipe, but in the absence of other advice, ensure that the open end is at least 600mm (2ft) above the floor.

Cut a hole through the wall to the outside and run the wastepipe to the gully, or attach it to a drainage stack with a strap boss (▷). Allow a minimum fall of 6mm (¼in) for every 300mm (1ft) of pipe run.

Anti-siphon devices

The standpipe and trap method of draining domestic appliances prevents back-siphonage by venting the pipe to the air. There are other ways of dealing with the problem, but you should check with your local water authority to ensure that such methods meet with their approval. If an existing 36 or 43mm (1¼ or 1½in) wastepipe runs behind the machine, you can attach a hose connector which incorporates a non-return valve to eliminate reverse flow. Connectors are available with short spigots (**1**) or as a standpipe. Double standpipes (**2**) permit two appliances to drain into the same connector.

Clamp the saddle over the wastepipe (**3**), then use the cutter supplied with the fitting to bore a hole in the pipe using the saddle as a guide (**4**).

You can drain a washing machine to a sink trap which has a built-in connector for the hose, but you should insert an in-line anti-siphon return valve in the appliance drain hose. It is a small plastic device with a hose connector at each end (**5**).

PREVENTING A FLOOD

Anyone who has had the misfortune of a flooded kitchen caused by a split hose or some mechanical breakdown within a machine will be only too aware of the possible extent of the damage. If the machine is unattended, water continues to flow at mains pressure, ruining floor coverings and furnishings. The consequences can be even worse if the machine is installed upstairs. Once the ceiling beneath becomes thoroughly waterlogged, it collapses, dumping the flood water into the room below.

An overflow safety valve, fitted into the supply, measures the amount of water passing through. If a fault occurs, and the volume of water exceeds a predetermined setting, the valve shuts off the supply immediately. The valve is set before installation to allow for the capacity of the machine it is monitoring plus a small safety margin to avoid excessive sensitivity. Setting instructions are provided by the manufacturer. If a flood occurs, some damage is inevitable, but the valve will avert a disaster. Once the fault is repaired, the valve is reset by pressing a button inside the outlet.

Attaching a machine hose to a safety valve

SEE ALSO

Details for: ▷	
Strap boss	34
Connecting pipes	20-27

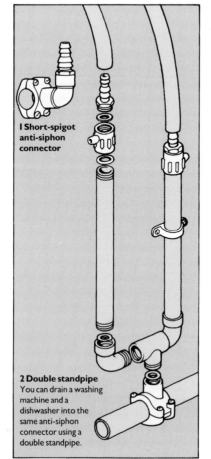

1 Short-spigot anti-siphon connector

2 Double standpipe
You can drain a washing machine and a dishwasher into the same anti-siphon connector using a double standpipe.

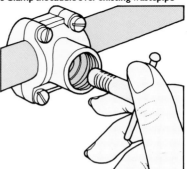

3 Clamp the saddle over existing wastepipe

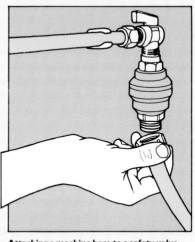

4 Bore a hole with the special cutter

5 An in-line anti-siphon hose valve

WATER SOFTENERS

Water treated at the local waterworks is rendered safe to drink in that all harmful impurities are removed before it is supplied to our houses. However, minerals absorbed from the ground before treatment are still present, and it is the concentration of these minerals which determines whether our water is hard or soft.

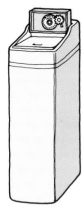

A typical domestic water softener

Rocky terrain gives rise to surface-run water which is naturally soft, but in areas of the country where water runs through the ground, rather than over it, a much higher dissolved mineral content produces slightly to very hard water. These impurities are not visible in tap water, but mineral salts are deposited in the form of hard scale on the inside of pipes, cisterns, and especially, hot water cylinders. If the concentration of minerals is very high, scale can eventually block pipework, and insulate heating elements to such an extent that their efficiency is reduced by anything from 15 to 70 per cent. The more obvious effects of hard water are the scumming and discoloration of baths and basins, blocked shower heads, blemished stainless steel surfaces and furred-up kettles. Most people learn to live with them, but all these effects can be reduced or even eliminated by installing a water softener.

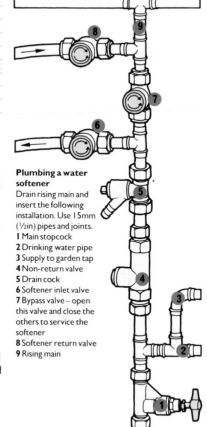

Plumbing a water softener
Drain rising main and insert the following installation. Use 15mm (½in) pipes and joints.
1 Main stopcock
2 Drinking water pipe
3 Supply to garden tap
4 Non-return valve
5 Drain cock
6 Softener inlet valve
7 Bypass valve – open this valve and close the others to service the softener
8 Softener return valve
9 Rising main

Domestic water softeners

Water softeners work on the principle of ion exchange. Incoming hard water flows through a compartment containing a synthetic resin which absorbs scale-forming calcium and magnesium ions and releases sodium ions in their place. After a period of two or three days, the resin is unable to absorb any more mineral salts at which time the softener automatically flushes the compartment with a saline solution to regenerate the resin. Topping up with granular salt is required at intervals of perhaps two to three months. Water softeners are fitted with a timer to programme regeneration for the early hours of the morning when water consumption is at its lowest.

The unit must be connected to the rising main at the point where it enters the house, which could be under the stairs, in the cellar or utility room, but more than likely in the kitchen. For this reason, softeners designed for average domestic use will fit under a standard kitchen worktop.

Installing a water softener

The installation of a water softener appears at first sight to be fairly complicated because it involves a great deal of joint making, firstly to include the valves and branch pipes to supply and bypass the softener, but also to include certain fittings to comply with water authority regulations.

The bypass assembly allows for the unit to be isolated for servicing while maintaining the supply of water to the rest of the house. In addition, you must install a branch pipe before the assembly to supply unsoftened drinking water to the kitchen sink. Supply a garden tap from the same pipe – there is no need to waste softened water on the garden.

Most water authorities will require a non-return valve in the system to prevent the reverse flow of salty water, and possibly a pressure reducing valve as well. You will also need a draincock to empty the rising main. Some manufacturers supply an installation kit which includes all the necessary equipment.

You will have to provide drainage in the form of a standpipe and trap as for a washing machine (▷).

Wire the softener to a switched, fused connection unit containing a 3 amp fuse (▷).

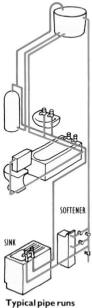

Typical pipe runs
A domestic system incorporating a softener.
Red:Hot water
Blue:Cold water

FITTING A GARDEN TAP

A tap situated on an outside wall is far more convenient than the kitchen sink for filling buckets or watering cans, and for attaching a hose for a lawn sprinkler or for washing the car.

Bib taps for garden installation are made with a threaded spout or push-on connector for a hose. The tap inlet screws into a wall plate.

Turn off the main stopcock and drain the rising main (◁). Fit a tee joint (1) in the rising main to run the supply to the tap. Connect a short length of pipe to a miniature valve (2). During the winter you can close this valve and run the garden tap to empty the pipe in case it should freeze. Continue with the pipework to the outside location, drilling a hole through the wall with a large masonry drill (3). Screw the wall plate compression joint onto the pipe (◁) but do not tighten it (4). Mark the wall plate fixing holes, then remove it to drill and plug the holes. Screw the plate

to the wall and tighten the compression joint. Wrap PTFE tape around the tap's threaded inlet (◁) and screw it into the wall plate (5). Turn on the supply and check for leaks.

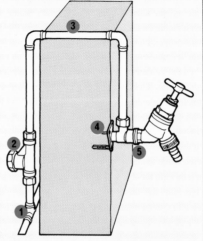

Pipes and fittings to supply a garden tap

STORAGE CISTERNS

The cold water storage cistern, normally situated in the roofspace, supplies the hot water cylinder and all the cold taps in the house other than the one used for drinking water in the kitchen. An old house may still be fitted with a heavy, galvanized steel cistern which has probably been in service since the house was built. Eventually it will corrode and although it can be patched up temporarily with an epoxy filler, it makes sense to replace it before a serious leak develops.

A circular, 227 litre (50 gallon) capacity, polythene cistern is the most popular choice as a replacement because it can be folded to pass through a narrow hatchway to the loft. It is also very much lighter and easier to handle than the old style cistern. Make sure the new cistern is supplied with a lid to keep the water clean.

Removing the old cistern

Switch off water-heating appliances, then close the stopcock on the rising main and drain the cistern by opening the bathroom cold taps.

Bail out the remaining water in the bottom of the cistern, then use a spanner to disconnect the fittings connecting the float valve, distribution pipes and overflow, to the cistern. Use a little penetrating oil if the fittings are stiff with corrosion. The cistern may have been built into the house before the roof was completed, so it is unlikely to pass through the loft hatch. In any case it is very cumbersome, so just pull it to one side.

Installing the new cistern

You may be able to use the existing fittings although the pipework is unlikely to fit the new cistern without some modification. If the fittings are badly corroded, buy new replacements.

Prepare a firm base for the cistern by nailing stout planks across the joists or build a platform with 18mm (¾in) thick chipboard or plywood.

PLUMBING A NEW CISTERN

Connecting the float valve
A float valve shuts off the supply of water from the rising main when the cistern is full (▷). Cut a hole for the float valve, 75mm (3in) below the top of the cistern. As a float valve is relatively heavy, some cisterns are supplied with a reinforcing plate to stiffen the plastic around the hole.

Slip a plastic washer onto the tail of the float valve and pass it through the hole. Place another washer and fixing nut on the outside, then tighten the fitting with two spanners.

Screw a tap connector (▷) onto the valve ready for connecting to the 15mm (½in) rising main.

Connecting the distribution pipes
The 22mm (¾in) pipes running to cylinder and cold taps are attached to the cistern with tank connectors – threaded inlets with a compression fitting (▷) for the pipework. Drill a hole for each tank connector about 50mm (2in) above the bottom of the cistern. Slip a connector, plus washer, through each hole from the inside, then tighten the fixing nut and washer on the outside to clamp the fitting to the cistern. The distribution pipes will be attached to the protruding spigots.

Take the opportunity to fit a gate valve (▷) to each distribution pipe so that you can cut off the supply of water without having to empty the cistern.

Connecting the overflow
Use a bent plastic tank connector for the overflow pipe. Drill a hole for it, 25mm (1in) below the level of the float valve inlet. Pass the connector through the hole and tighten its fixing nut on the inside of the cistern.

Attach a 21mm (¾in) plastic overflow pipe to the connector using its compression fitting. Run the pipe to the floor, then to the outside of the house maintaining a continuous fall. The pipe must emerge in a conspicuous position so that an overflow can be detected immediately. Clip the overflow to the roof timbers.

Connecting the plumbing
Modify the rising main and distribution pipes to align with their fittings then connect them with compression fittings (▷). (Don't use soldered joints near a plastic cistern.) Clip all the pipework securely to the joists.

Open the main stopcock and check for leaks as the cistern fills. As the water level approaches the top, adjust the float arm to maintain the level 25mm (1in) below the overflow outlet (▷).

There is a hole in the lid to accommodate the vent pipe from the hot water cylinder (▷). Either adapt the pipe to pass through the hole, or drop a plastic funnel into the hole to catch the water discharged from the pipe. Finally, insulate the cistern and pipework (▷).

SEE ALSO

Details for: ▷	
Insulation	65
Float valves	13-14
Tap connector	14
Adjusting float arm	14
Gate valve	20
Compression joint	22
Cylinder	48

Tank cutters
Hire a tank cutter to bore holes in a cistern for pipework. Some cutters are adjustable to drill holes of different diameters. Alternatively, use a hole saw clamped to a drill.

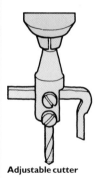

Adjustable cutter

Hole saw

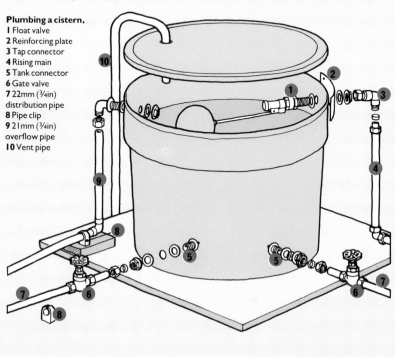

Plumbing a cistern.
1 Float valve
2 Reinforcing plate
3 Tap connector
4 Rising main
5 Tank connector
6 Gate valve
7 22mm (¾in) distribution pipe
8 Pipe clip
9 21mm (¾in) overflow pipe
10 Vent pipe

REPLACING A HOT WATER CYLINDER

The hot water in most houses is heated and stored in a large copper cylinder situated in the airing cupboard. Cold water is fed to the base of the cylinder from the storage cistern in the loft. As the water is heated, it rises to the top of the cylinder where it is drawn off via the vent pipe to the hot taps.

Packaged plumbing
In an apartment, the cistern might be mounted in a frame over the cylinder (1), or both might be built into a single casing (2).

Direct systems
Heating may be accomplished with electric immersion heaters only. A single or double element heater is fitted into the top of the cylinder, or there may be two individual side entry heaters (◁). On the other hand, the water may be heated in a boiler with the sole purpose of providing hot water for the cylinder. A cold water pipe runs from the base of the cylinder, to the boiler where it is heated and returns to the top half of the cylinder. Both methods are known as direct systems. In reality, a boiler-heated cylinder is usually fitted with an immersion heater as well to supply hot water during the summer months when the boiler would make the kitchen or utility room uncomfortably warm.

Indirect system
When a house is centrally heated with radiators fed by a boiler (◁), the water in the cylinder is normally heated indirectly by a heat exchanger. Hot water from the boiler passes through the exchanger, a coiled tube within the cylinder, where the heat is transmitted to the stored water. The heat exchanger is part of a completely self-contained system with its own small storage cistern in the loft which tops up the system. A vent pipe terminates open-ended over the same small cistern. The whole system is known as the primary circuit, and the pipes running from and back to the boiler are known as the primary flow and return. An indirect system might be supplemented by an immersion heater.

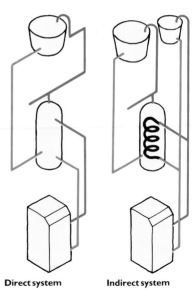

Direct system　　　Indirect system

Typical pipe runs
Red:Hot water
Blue:Cold water

1 Frame-mounted cistern

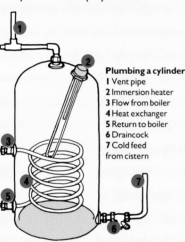

2 Cased cistern and cylinder

CYLINDERS

The capacity of domestic cylinders ranges from 114 litres (25 gallons) to about 227 litres (50 gallons) although there are bigger cylinders to meet the requirements of large families. A cylinder with a capacity of between 182 and 227 litres (40 and 50 gallons) will store enough hot water to satisfy the needs of an average family for a whole day. Many cylinders are made from thin, uninsulated copper. They need a thick lagging jacket to reduce heat loss, but there is a growing preference for factory-insulated cylinders covered with a layer of foamed polyurethane.

Plumbing a cylinder
1 Vent pipe
2 Immersion heater
3 Flow from boiler
4 Heat exchanger
5 Return to boiler
6 Draincock
7 Cold feed from cistern

Changing a cylinder

You may wish to replace an existing cylinder because it has sprung a leak, or because a larger one will allow you to take full advantage of economical night time electricity by storing more cheap hot water (◁). A simple replacement can be achieved without modifying the plumbing but you will have to adapt the pipework to fit a larger cylinder.

Drain the pipework and cylinder (◁). Disconnect any immersion heaters from the electrical supply (◁). Then use a special spanner available from a tool hire outlet to unscrew them. Disconnect all the pipework, springing it out of the way while you remove the cylinder.

Place the new cylinder in position and check the pipework for alignment. Modify the pipes as necessary (◁), then make the connections using PTFE tape to make sure the threaded joints are watertight (◁). Take the opportunity to fit a draincock to the supply pipe from the cistern (◁).

With the rubber sealing washer in place, wrap PTFE tape around the thread of an immersion heater and screw it into the cylinder. Reconnect it to the electrical supply (◁), then fill the system and check for leaks before attempting to heat the water. Check for leaks again when the water is up to temperature, and if all is well, lag the cylinder and pipework (◁).

INSTANTANEOUS WATER HEATERS

Instantaneous water heaters provide hot water at the point it is required – over the sink or hand basin. When you turn the tap, the flow of water activates a powerful electric heater, or ignites the burner in the case of a gas appliance. (Gas water heaters should be installed by a qualified fitter.)

Electric heaters are supplied with water from the rising main with 15mm (½in) pipework connected to the water inlet just below the tap with a standard compression fitting (◁).

A 3kW model, suitable for a basin, is wired to a fused connection unit containing a 13 amp fuse (◁). Use a 7kW heater over a sink. That requires a 30 amp circuit like a shower but in a kitchen you can use a wall-mounted double pole switch to connect it instead of a ceiling-mounted switch (◁).

Connecting a 3kW heater
1 Fused connection unit
2 15mm (½in) supply pipe

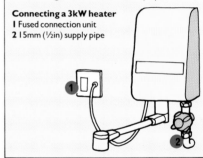

WET CENTRAL HEATING

The most popular form of central heating is the wet system in which water is heated by a boiler and pumped through small-bore pipes to radiators or to convector heaters, where the heat from the water is released into the rooms. The water circulates back to the boiler for reheating in a continuing cycle.

The control of such a system can be extremely flexible. Thermostats and valves allow the output of individual heat emitters to be automatically adjusted, and parts of the system can be shut down if rooms are unoccupied.

An extra advantage of the wet system is that it can be used to heat the hot water supply for the house as well as heating the house itself.

The boiler for wet central heating may be heated by gas, oil, bottled gas (propane), solid fuel such as anthracite, or electricity.

SEE ALSO

Details for: ▷	
Insulation	77
Off-peak electricity	71
Hot water cylinders	48

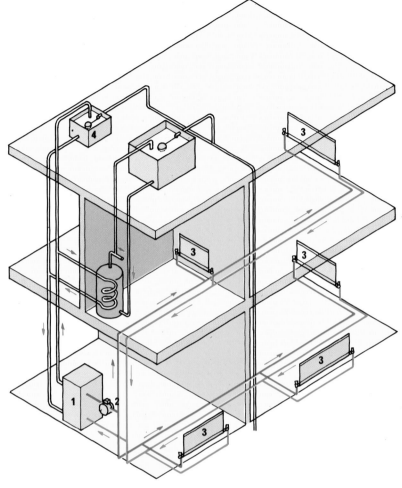

Two-pipe central heating system ▶

The water, heated by the boiler (1), is forced by the pump (2) through the pipes to the various radiators or special convector heaters (3) which hold it long enough for it to warm the rooms before it returns to the boiler to be reheated.

A cistern (4) in the roof keeps the system topped up and catches any expansion of the water due to overheating.

Red indicates the flow of water from the pump; blue shows the return flow.

One-pipe systems

A one-pipe system has a single large-bore pipe running around the perimeter of a house, forming a loop. The flow and return pipes of each radiator are connected to this large-bore pipe. The water is pumped round the loop but the radiators work by gravity circulation. Larger radiators may be used at the end of the loop to compensate for heat loss. The cistern and hot water circuits are the same as on a two-pipe system.

COMPARATIVE RUNNING COSTS

The running costs of the various central heating systems vary with local costs of fuel, the fuel chosen, the type of system, the size of the house and how well the house is insulated. Here it must be stressed that whatever kind of central heating you install you will make considerable savings if you take steps to insulate the house properly beforehand (▷). By drastically reducing the amount of heat you lose through your walls, roof, windows and doors you will also reduce the size of the heating system you need. This means substantial saving on your capital outlay as well as on subsequent running costs. A good central heating designer/installer takes account of the quality of the insulation in a house when making his calculations of the heat required.

When you're choosing your heating system you should carefully bear in mind the availability of the various fuels. Solid fuel, oil and electricity are available to every household, though note that the first two need some kind of storage facility and this may not be easy to arrange. Mains gas supply is not available everywhere, though even then, if you particularly want gas, you could opt for the bottled kind. In this case a storage facility is also needed – either a large tank or some kind of housing for several large cyiinders.

The efficiency of the heat source also has an effect on overall running costs. A proportion of the heat generated by gas, oil and solid-fuel boilers is lost up the flue, only some 65 per cent getting through the system and warming the house. Off-peak electric storage heaters and boilers, whatever their drawbacks, are much more efficient, with a usable heat closer to 95 per cent of that which is generated.

When it comes to running costs there is generally little to choose between gas, solid fuel and off-peak electricity, though at the higher heat levels gas comes out marginally cheaper. Oil prices fluctuate a great deal and on average oil works out about 1 1/2 times as dear as the other three. Bottled gas is even dearer, as is daytime-rate as opposed to off-peak electricity.

On balance, mains gas is probably the best fuel if it is available. It is clean, it offers infinitely controllable heat-output, it needs no storage and its supply is always secure.

CENTRAL HEATING BOILERS

The boiler is the heart of any wet central heating system, and modern ones are compact and very efficient. They can be gas- or oil-fired, can burn solid fuels like anthracite or can run on cheap off-peak electric power. Maintained properly, such a boiler will give you years of trouble-free service.

POSITIONING A BOILER

Modern central heating boilers are fairly easy to accommodate. Whether fired by oil, gas or solid fuel they are manufactured with neat, well-designed casings that blend in with ordinary kitchen or utility room furniture. Some gas-fired versions can be mounted high on walls, where they take up no more space than most kitchen cabinets.

Gas- and oil-fired boilers are available with a choice of conventional flues or balanced flues. Those with conventional flues are freestanding, designed for connection to an existing chimney or to a new prefabricated one. Balanced-flue boilers don't need a chimney. Their flue gases are passed along a short horizontal duct through an outside wall. The duct is split into two passages, one for the outgoing flue gases and the other for incoming combustion air drawn into the boiler from outside the house. Boilers with balanced flues are sometimes called 'room sealed' because they take no air from the room where they are sited, only from the outside.

Balanced-flue boilers can be fitted anywhere in the house so long as the site is on or next to an outside wall. Under stairs can be an ideal position.

Both gas and solid-fuel boilers offer a further choice, that of having the boiler – fitted as a back boiler behind a radiant fire or room heater (◁) – sited in the living room fireplace. In the case of gas the control of the radiant fire is independent of the boiler, and you can operate one or the other or both, as you wish according to the season.

Electrically heated boilers are completely versatile in the matter of siting. They can be placed anywhere convenient, since they have no flues and need no connection to the air outside the house.

All solid-fuel boilers must be connected to chimneys.

Gas-fired boilers

Most gas-fired boilers have pilot lights that burn constantly and light the burners when heat is required. They can work manually or by a timer set to switch the heating on and off at times you choose. You can also link the boiler to a room thermostat so that the heating is switched on and off to keep the temperatures even throughout the house. Another thermostat, in the boiler itself, prevents the water overheating at any time.

Some boilers have electronic ignition by which the pilot light ignites only when a thermostat demands heat. Once the boiler temperature is right, valves to the burner and pilot close until the next time heat is called for.

Oil-fired boilers

Oil-fired boilers, with the same efficient controls as gas-fired ones, come in two basic types: pressure jet and vaporizing. This refers to whether the oil is reduced to tiny droplets or turned into vapour to be burnt. Pressure-jet boilers are too noisy for use indoors and must be housed outside. Vaporizing boilers are much quieter. A drawback of any oil-fired boiler is the need for a large storage tank for the oil, sited outside for easy access by the delivery tanker.

Solid-fuel boilers

Solid-fuel heating also needs a suitable place for fuel storage, and as these boilers produce a considerable amount of ash it has to be removed every day.

The rate at which the solid fuel is burnt is usually controlled by a thermostatic damper, sometimes by a fan. The instant switching on and off of the heat – as with gas- and oil-fired boilers – is not possible, and the system must have some way for heat to escape in the event of the water-circulating pump failing; otherwise the water could boil in the appliance and damage it. This is usually arranged by means of a 'natural convection' pipe circuit between the boiler and the heat exchanger in the domestic hot-water cylinder, or a radiator in the bathroom, where the excess heat can be used to dry towels.

A solid-fuel boiler must be kept well stoked if it is to continue burning, and you can have one with a hopper feed that will top it up automatically while you are out of the house.

● **Room heaters**
Gas or solid-fuel heaters with built-in back boilers provide local warmth when the central heating is shut down in the spring or early autumn. To provide yourself with a source of 'instant' heat, choose a gas heater. Consider an electric immersion heater for summer hot water.

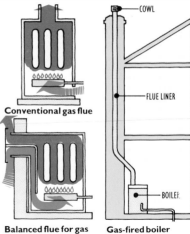

Conventional gas flue

Balanced flue for gas

Gas-fired boiler

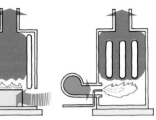

Vaporizing boiler

Pressure-jet boiler

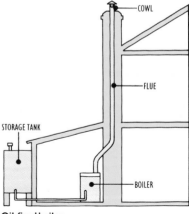

Oil-fired boiler

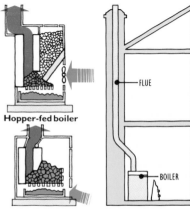

Hopper-fed boiler

Solid-fuel back boiler

Solid-fuel boiler

BOILER CAPACITY

Deciding what boiler capacity you'll need is not a matter of guesswork, however intelligent, but of complicated mathematical calculations that will determine accurately the total heat requirement of the house. A designer/installer of heating systems will take all the following items into account:

The size of the house; the type of house; its position; the number of rooms it has; the temperature needed in each room, based on a standard outdoor temperature; the method of its construction; the materials of the walls, floors, ceilings and roof; and the level of thermal insulation installed.

Working out your needs
From this information the designer can work out the size of the heat-emitters needed, and by adding up their outputs he will arrive at the total output needed from the boiler. Boiler outputs are quoted in British thermal units per hour (Btu/h) or kilowatts (kW); 10,000 Btu/h equals 3kW.

So many variables are involved that it is impossible to make calculations for every possible combination of them.

The best course when you consider installing a heating system is to get quotes from several designers for installing it. Each of them should produce a detailed rundown of the kind of equipment needed, and the sizes of radiators and boiler, together with an estimate of the cost of the installation. If they have done their jobs properly their figures for your heat requirements should be very similar. If the estimates show substantial differences you should ask for a further explanation of how the figures were arrived at.

If you already have central heating and wish to replace an old boiler you must get one with the same heat output as the original one, unless you plan to extend the system, in which case consult a designer/installer as you would about a new system.

Getting expert approval
When you set out to buy a boiler be sure that it has the approval of the relevant body – for gas: British Gas; for oil: Domestic Oil Burning Equipment Testing Association (DOBETA); for solid fuel: the Solid Fuel Advisory Service or the Solid Smokeless Fuels Federation; for electricity: the Electricity Board.

RADIATORS AND CONVECTORS

The hot water from a central heating boiler is pumped through the house along narrow pipes which may be connected to radiators or to special convector heaters (▷) that extract heat from the water and pass it out into their respective rooms.

You can feel radiant heat being emitted directly from the hot surface of an appliance, but convected heat warms the air that comes into contact with the hot surface. As the warmed air rises toward the ceiling it allows cooler air to flow in round the appliance, and this air in its turn is warmed and moves upwards. Eventually a steady but very gentle circulation of air takes place in the room, and the temperature gradually rises to the optimum set on the room thermostat.

SEE ALSO
Details for: ▷
Convectors   52

Radiators

An ordinary radiator is a double-skinned metal panel. Water flows into it through a manually adjustable valve at one corner and then out through a lockshield valve at the other. A bleed valve is fitted to one of the top corners to let air out and prevent airlocks, which stop the radiator heating up properly. The faces of most radiators are fluted to increase their surface area for greater heat output.

Despite the name, radiators deliver only about half of their output as radiant heat; the rest is emitted through natural convection as the surrounding air comes into contact with the hot surfaces of the radiators.

Radiators come in a wide range of sizes, and the larger they are the greater is their heat output. Heat output can be further increased by using special double- or even triple-panel radiators whose panels are mounted one behind the other. There are also some radiators with finned rear faces to step up the output of convected heat.

Single-panel radiator

Double-panel radiator

Finned radiator

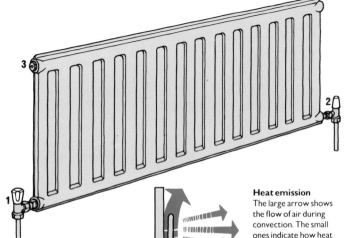

Panel radiator
1 The manual valve controls inflow
2 The lockshield valve controls outflow to keep the radiator hot
3 The bleed valve is to disperse airlocks

Heat emission
The large arrow shows the flow of air during convection. The small ones indicate how heat radiates from the radiator's surface.

CONVECTORS

You can fit convector heaters into your wet central heating system instead of the rather more conventional radiators.

Unlike radiators, convector heaters emit none of their heat in the form of direct radiation. The hot water from the boiler passes through a finned pipe inside the heater, the fins absorbing the heat and transferring it to the air surrounding them. The warmed air escapes through an opening at the top of the appliance and at the same time cool air is drawn in through the open bottom, to be warmed in its turn.

Most convector heaters have a damper that can be set to control the airflow. Some are designed for inconspicuous fixing at skirting level. An advance is a fan-assisted type in which the airflow over the heating fins is forced, making for fast room heating.

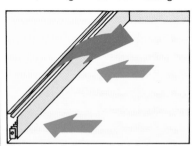
Rising warm air draws cool air in below

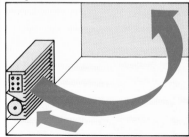
Airflow by fan-assisted convection

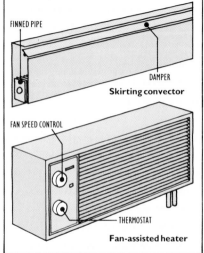
FINNED PIPE

DAMPER
Skirting convector

FAN SPEED CONTROL

THERMOSTAT
Fan-assisted heater

PLACING YOUR HEATERS

At one time central heating radiators or convectors were nearly always placed under windows to balance the chill of the panes and cut the draughts caused by warmed air cooling against them. If double glazing deals with both of these problems you can place them with an eye to maximum comfort – but keep the other on the length and consequent cost of pipe runs.

Convenience and cost

Your radiators and convector heaters can be positioned anywhere that's convenient, that suits the shape of the rooms and that keeps costly pipe runs to a reasonable minimum. Probably you'll want to take all of these considerations into account.

While double glazing means that the appliances can be sited elsewhere than under windows there is a slight drawback to placing them against walls. The warm air rising from them will tend to discolour the paint or wallpaper above. You can guard against this by fitting radiator shelves immediately above them to direct the warm air clear of the walls.

Never hang curtains or stand furniture in front of radiators or convectors. Either will absorb radiated heat and curtains will trap convected heat between themselves and the walls. While convectors radiate almost no heat you should never obstruct warm air leaving the appliance nor cool air being drawn into it.

A room's shape can affect the siting of appliances and perhaps their number. For example, you cannot heat a large L-shaped room from a radiator in its short end. A heating installer can work out a combination of appliances – and their positions – to heat the room properly.

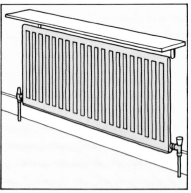
A shelf directs warm air clear of the wall

Selecting the size of heaters

A house loses heat constantly – whenever a door or window is opened; because of cold draughts; through the fabric of the doors, windows, walls, floors, ceilings and roof. To work out the heating needs of the rooms in a house the designer has to take account of the rate at which they lose heat. This varies with the materials and construction of the walls, floors and ceilings. For example, heat is lost more quickly through a solid brick wall than through a brick cavity wall with cavity insulation. Also the temperatures on the other sides of walls, floors and ceilings will come into the equation.

The designer also needs to know the temperature to which each room must be heated, and there are standard levels for particular rooms (See right). The designer's calculations will produce a heating requirement for each room, expressed in kilowatts, and the next step is to select radiators or convectors of appropriate outputs. Then all the heat output figures are totalled to give the output required from the boiler.

When you install your central heating be sure to choose radiators and convector heaters that carry the sign of approval of the Manufacturers' Association for Radiators and Convectors (MARC).

IDEAL ROOM TEMPERATURES

A central heating designer/installer aims at a system that will heat rooms to the temperatures shown here, assuming an outdoor temperature of -1°C (30°F).

ROOM	TEMPERATURE
Living room	21°C (70°F)
Dining room	21°C (70°F)
Kitchen	16°C (60°F)
Hall/landing	18°C (65°F)
Bedroom	16°C (60°F)
Bathroom	23°C (72°F)

CENTRAL HEATING CONTROLS

A range of automatic control systems and devices for wet central heating can, if used sensibly, enable you to make useful savings in running costs. They can ensure that your system never 'burns up money' by producing unwanted heat.

Three basic devices

While considerable sophistication is now available in automatic control the systems can be divided into three main types: temperature controllers (thermostats), automatic on-off switches (timers and programmers) and heating circuit controllers (zone valves).

These devices can be used individually or in combination to provide a very high level of control.

It must be added that automatic controls are really effective only with gas- or oil-fired boilers, which can be switched on and off at will. Linked to solid-fuel boilers, which take time to react to controls, the systems will be less effective and can be dangerous.

ZONE CONTROL VALVES

It is not often that all the rooms in a house are in use at once. During the day it is normal for the upstairs rooms to be unused for long periods, and to heat them permanently would be very wasteful. To avoid such waste you can divide your central heating system into circuits, or zones – the usual ones being upstairs and downstairs – and heat those areas only when it's necessary.

Control is provided by motorized valves linked to a timer or programmer that directs the flow of heating water through pre-selected pipes at the pre-selected times. Alternatively zone valves can be used to provide zone temperature control by being linked to individual zone thermostats.

A motorized zone control valve

Thermostats

All boilers incorporate thermostats to prevent overheating. A gas- or oil-fired boiler will have one that can be set to alter heat output by switching the unit on and off. On a solid-fuel boiler the thermostat opens and closes a damper, allowing more or less air to the firebed to increase or reduce the rate of burning as required.

Room thermostats – 'roomstats' for short – are common forms of central heating control, often the only ones fitted. They are placed in rooms where temperatures usually remain fairly stable, and work on the assumption that any rise or drop in room temperatures will be matched by similar ones through the house. Roomstats control temperatures through simple on-off switching of the boiler – or the pump if a boiler must run constantly to provide a constant supply of domestic hot water.

The roomstat's drawback is that it can make no allowance for local temperature changes in other rooms caused, for example, by the sun shining through a window or a separate heater being switched on. Much more sophisticated temperature control is provided by thermostatic radiator valves, which can be fitted to radiators instead of the standard manually operated inlet valves. Temperature sensors open and close them, varying heat output to maintain the desired temperatures in individual rooms.

Thermostatic radiator valves need not be fitted in every room. You can use one to reduce the heat in a kitchen or reduce the temperature in a bathroom while using a roomstat to regulate the temperature in the rest of the house or upstairs and downstairs zones.

Other available thermostatic controls include devices for regulating the temperature of domestic hot water and for giving frost-protection to a boiler switched off during winter holidays.

Timers and programmers

You can save a lot in running costs by ensuring that your heating system is not working when you don't need it – while you're out, for instance, or while you sleep. A timer can be set to switch the system on and off so as to suit the regular comings and goings of the family. It can switch on and warm the house just before you get up, then off again just before you leave for work, on again while you're coming home, and so on.

The simpler timers offer two 'on' and two 'off' settings which are repeated daily, though a manual override allows variations for weekends and such times. More sophisticated versions, known as programmers, offer a large number of on-off programmes – even a different one for each day of the week – as well as control of domestic hot water.

SEE ALSO

Details for: ▷
Boilers   50

Timer

Roomstat

Programmer

Thermostatic radiator valve

Heating controls
There are several ways to control the temperature of central heating.
1 Programmer controls boiler and pump.
2 A timer is used to control a zone valve. It can be used to regulate boiler and pump in place of a programmer.
3 Roomstat controls pump or a zone valve.
4 A non-electrical radiator valve controls an individual heater.

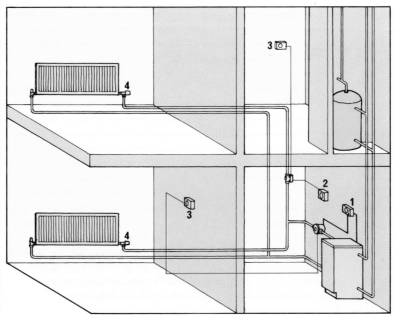

HEATING SYSTEM FAULTFINDER

SYMPTOM

Hissing or banging sounds from boiler or pipework.

Overheating caused by:

- Blocked chimney (with solid fuel).
  Check flueway for substantial soot fall. Sweep chimney (◁).

- Heavy scale deposits in system due to hard water.
  Shut down boiler and pump. Have a specialist treat system with a descaler, then drain, flush and refill system.

- Faulty boiler thermostat.
  Shut down boiler.
  Leave pump working to circulate water round system and cool it quickly. With system cool, operate boiler thermostat control. If you do not hear a clicking sound call in an engineer.

- Lack of water in system
  Shut down boiler.
  Check feed and expansion cistern in roof. If empty, the valve may be stuck. Move ball valve float arm up and down to restore flow and fill system. If this fails, with valve in open position check whether mains water has been turned off by accident or – in winter – whether supply pipe is frozen.

- Circulating pump not working (with solid fuel).
  Shut down boiler, then check that the pump is switched on.
  If pump won't work turn off power and check wired connections to it. If pump seems to be running but outlet pipe is cool, check for airlock by using bleed screw. If pump is still not working shut it down, drain system, remove pump and check it for blockage. Clean pump or replace it if necessary.

SYMPTOM

Continuous drip from overflow pipe of feed and expansion cistern in roof.

- Faulty ball valve or leaking float that keeps valve open.
  Shut off mains water supply to cistern and bale cistern out to below level of valve. Remove valve and fit new washer (◁). Alternatively unscrew leaking float from arm and fit new one.

SYMPTOM

All radiators remain cool though boiler is operating normally.

- Pump not working
  Check that pump is working by feeling for motor vibration or by listening. If pump is running check for airlock by operating bleed valve. If this has no effect the pump outlet may be blocked. Switch off boiler and pump, remove pump and clean or replace as necessary.

- Pump's thermostat or timer is set incorrectly or is faulty.
  Check thermostat or timer setting and reset if necessary. If this makes no difference switch off power and check wiring connections. If connections are in good order call in an engineer.

SYMPTOM

Radiators in one part of the house do not warm up.

- Timer or thermostat which controls zone valve not set properly or faulty.
  Check timer or thermostat setting and reset if necessary. If this has no effect switch off the power supply and check wired connections. If this makes no difference call in an engineer.

- Zone valve itself faulty.
  Drain system and replace valve.

SYMPTOM

Single radiator does not warm up.

- Manual inlet valve closed.
  Check setting of valve and open it if that is necessary.

- Thermostatic radiator valve not set properly or faulty.
  Check setting of valve and reset it if necessary. If this has no effect drain system and replace valve (◁).

- Lockshield valve not set properly.
  Remove lockshield cover and adjust valve setting until radiator seems as warm as those in adjacent rooms. Have lockshield valve properly balanced when system is next serviced.

- Inlet/outlet blocked by corrosion.
  Close inlet and lockshield valves,

remove radiator and flush out and refit or replace as necessary.

SYMPTOM

Area at top of radiator stays cool while the bottom is warm.

- Airlock at top of radiator preventing water circulating fully.
  Operate bleed valve to release the trapped air (◁).

SYMPTOM

Cool patch in centre of radiator while top and ends are warm.

- Heavy deposits of corrosion at bottom of radiator are restricting circulation of water.
  Close inlet and lockshield valves, remove radiator, flush out, then refit or replace as necessary (◁).

SYMPTOM

Water leaking from system.

- Loose pipe unions at joints, pump connections, boiler connections, etc.
  Switch off boiler – or close down solid-fuel appliance, raking out coals – switch off pump and tighten leaking joints. If this has no effect drain the system and remake joints completely (◁).

- Split or punctured pipes.
  Wrap damage in rags temporarily, switch off boiler and pump and make a temporary repair with hose or commercial leak sealant (◁). Drain system and fit new pipe (◁).

SYMPTOM

Boiler not working

- Thermostat set too low
  Check roomstat or boiler thermostat is set correctly
- Timer or programmer not working
  Check the unit is switched on and set correctly. Have it replaced if the fault persists.
- Pilot light goes out
  Relight a gas boiler pilot light following the manufacturer's instructions, which are usually found on the back of the boiler's front panel. If the pilot fails to ignite, have the unit replaced.

DRAINING AND FILLING A WET SYSTEM

There may be times when you will have to drain your wet central heating system completely and refill it – during routine maintenance, when dealing with a fault *(See opposite) or if you decide to extend the system or upgrade the boiler. The job can be done fairly easily if you follow the procedures outlined here.*

Draining the system

Before draining your central heating system cool the water by shutting off the boiler and leaving the pump running. The circulating water will cool quickly.

Switch off the pump and turn off the mains water supply to the feed and expansion cistern in the roof by closing the stopcock in the feedpipe or by laying a batten across the cistern and tying the float arm to it to keep the ball valve shut.

The main draincock for the system will be in the return pipe near the boiler. Push one end of a garden hose onto its outlet, lead the other end of the hose to a gully or soakaway in the garden and open the draincock. If you have no key for its square shank use an adjustable spanner.

Water will drain from the system, but some will be held in the radiators by vacuum. To release this start at the top of the house and carefully open the radiator bleed valves. Air will flow into the tops of the radiators, breaking the vacuums, and the water will drain out.

Work down through the house, allowing time for the water to drain away, until the bleed valves on all radiators are open and the water has stopped flowing. Watch out for inverted pipe loops (See below).

Draining procedure
Turn off the mains supply to the cistern at the feedpipe stopcock (**1**). If there's no stopcock tie the ball valve float arm to a batten laid across the cistern (**2**). With a hose on the main draincock (**3**) and its other end at a gully or soakaway outside, open the draincock and let the system empty. Release any water trapped in radiators (**4**) by opening their bleed valves (**5**), starting at the top of the house. Be sure to close all draincocks before you refill the system.

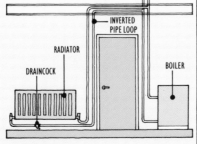

INVERTED PIPE LOOPS

When fitting a central heating system in a house with solid ground floors the installer will run the pipes from the boiler into the ceiling void and drop them down to the individual radiators. Each of these 'inverted pipe loops' has its own draincock. They must be drained separately after the main system has been emptied.

An inverted pipe loop has its own draincock

REFILLING THE SYSTEM

Before you refill the system check that you have closed all the draincocks and radiator bleed valves. Restore the water supply to the feed and expansion cistern in the roof. As the system fills up, air will be trapped in the tops of the radiators, so when the water stops running bleed each radiator in turn, starting at the bottom of the house and working upwards (▷). You may also have to bleed the circulating pump (▷).

Finally check all the draincocks and bleed valves for signs of leakage and tighten them where necessary.

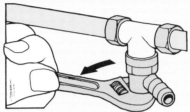

Tightening up a leaking draincock

PROTECTING THE SYSTEM

Using corrosion inhibitor

Any wet central heating system will suffer from corrosion to some extent. It is due not only to rust but also to a black sludge caused by a chemical reaction between the water, the steel radiators and the copper pipework. If it is allowed to build up it can clog the circulating pump and partially block radiators, reducing their heat output.

You can slow down corrosion by adding a proprietary corrosion inhibitor to the water. This is best done when the system is first installed, but the inhibitor can be introduced into the system at any later time. If the system has been running for some time it is better to flush it out first by draining and refilling it repeatedly until the water runs clean. Otherwise all you need to do is to drain off enough water to empty the feed and expansion cistern and a small amount of pipework – about 20 litres (4 gallons) – pour the inhibitor into the cistern and restore the water supply, which will carry the inhibitor into the pipework. About 5 litres (1 gallon) will be enough for most systems, but check the maker's instructions. Finally switch on the circulating pump to distribute the inhibitor round the system.

SEE ALSO

Details for: ▷	
Bleeding radiators	57
Bleeding pump	60
Gully	7, 17
Turning off water	8

BOILER MAINTENANCE

SEE ALSO
◁ Details for:
Switching off electricity   66

Regular cleaning and maintenance will give your central heating boiler a longer life and keep it efficient.

Gas- and oil-fired boilers should be serviced once a year by qualified engineers, but you can do a certain amount of cleaning on an oil-fired one.

Solid-fuel boilers need virtually no maintenance other than regular cleaning, which you can do yourself.

Solid-fuel boilers

If you have a solid-fuel system it is very important to keep the chimney and flueway swept. The job, which should be done twice a year, is done in the same way as for an open fire, access being through the front of a room heater with back boiler or through a soot door in the flue pipe or the chimney breast.

When you have swept the chimney, clean out the boiler with a stiff brush and take up the dust and soot particles with your vacuum cleaner.

Lift out any broken fire bars and drop new ones in place.

Oil-fired boilers

● **Sweeping chimney**
Hire chimney-sweep brushes or a special vacuum cleaner to remove soot deposits from a solid-fuel boiler flue. If it has not been swept for some time, use brushes as the vacuum is not suitable for heavy deposits. Insert the first length of cane with brush attached, and screw on additional lengths as you push the brush up the flue. When the brush emerges from the top of the chimney (you will feel the sudden lack of resistance) pull it back down, unscrewing canes as they emerge.

If you have an oil-fired boiler you should clean its walls and oil filter twice a year. The method you use will depend on whether the boiler is the vaporizing or pressure-jet type. Disconnect the electricity supply to the boiler and shut off the oil supply valve. Remove the boiler casing and the furnace cover plate.

Cover the burner of the vaporizing type. The side-entry pressure-jet nozzle will not usually need covering but you can block its draught tube with a rag. Clean the sides of the furnace with a wire brush, then remove the covers and extract the debris with your vacuum cleaner. Also use the vacuum cleaner to remove the dust in the casing.

Place a drip tray under the filter unit before removing the filter element. The vaporizing boiler has an oil-level control valve incorporating a filter. Unscrew the drain plug and remove the filter element (1). Wash it in petrol, shake dry and replace. The pressure-jet boiler has an in-line filter. Unscrew the retaining bolt (2) and remove the filter bowl. Clean out the bowl and wash or replace the filter before reassembly.

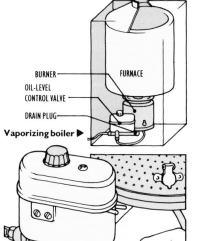

BURNER — FURNACE
OIL-LEVEL
CONTROL VALVE
DRAIN PLUG
Vaporizing boiler ▶

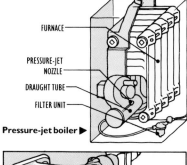

FURNACE
PRESSURE-JET
NOZZLE
DRAUGHT TUBE
FILTER UNIT
Pressure-jet boiler ▶

1 Unscrew drain plug and remove the filter

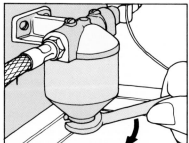

2 Slacken the bolt with a spanner

Gas-fired boilers

If your central heating system is gas-fired there is very little that you can do in the way of maintenance. The job – as for other gas appliances – is one for the professionals (See right).

But you can ensure that the interior is kept free of dust and fluff. This is important especially round the jets.

PROFESSIONAL SERVICING SCHEMES

The very high efficiency of modern gas- and oil-fired boilers largely depends on their being regularly checked and serviced. It should be done annually, and because the mechanisms involved are so complex the work should be done by qualified engineers.

For either type of boiler you can enter into a contract – with either the original installer or the fuel supplier – for regular maintenance.

Gas-fired installations

British Gas offer a choice of several servicing schemes for gas-fired boilers. These cover their own installations, but they can sometimes be arranged for systems put in by other installers on condition a British Gas inspection of the installation is carried out.

The simplest of the British Gas schemes provides for an annual check and adjustment of the boiler. If any repairs are found to be necessary, either at the time of the regular check or at other times during the year, the labour and the required parts will be charged separately. But for an extra fee it is possible to have both free labour and free parts for boiler repairs at any time of the year. British Gas will also extend the arrangement to include a check of the whole heating system at the same time as the boiler is being checked.

It may be that your own installer can offer you a similar choice of servicing schemes. The best course is to compare the charges and decide which gives the best value for money.

Oil-fired installations

The installers of oil-fired central heating systems and the suppliers of fuel oil offer servicing schemes similar to those outlined above for gas-fired systems. The choice of schemes ranges from the simple check-up each year to complete cover for new parts and labour if and when any repairs should become necessary.

Again, as with the schemes for gas, it is wisest to shop round and make a comparison of the various services on offer and the charges for them.

BLEEDING RADIATORS AND FITTING A BLEED VALVE

If a radiator feels cooler at the top than at the bottom it's likely that a pocket of air has formed in it and is stopping full circulation of the water. Getting the air out – 'bleeding' – is a simple matter.

Opening a bleed valve

Turn off the circulating pump, and preferably the boiler too, though this isn't vital.

Each radiator has a bleed valve at one of its top corners, identifiable by a square-section shank in the centre of the round blanking plug. You should have been given a key to fit these shanks by the installer, but if you weren't, or if you have inherited an old system, you can buy one at a good DIY shop or ironmonger's.

Use the key to turn the shank of the valve anti-clockwise about a quarter of a turn. It shouldn't be necessary to turn it further but have a small container handy to catch any spurting water if you do open the valve too far.

You will hear a hissing sound as the air escapes. Keep the key on the shank of the valve and when the hissing stops and the first dribble of water appears close the valve tightly.

In no circumstances must you be tempted to open the valve any more than is needed to let the air out, or to remove it completely, as this will produce a deluge of water.

Dispersing the air pocket in a radiator

Radiator key
Keep your radiator key in a handy place where you can find it at short notice. There is no substitute for it.

Fitting an automatic bleed valve

If you find yourself having to bleed one particular radiator regularly it will save you trouble if you replace its bleed valve with an automatic one that will allow air to escape but not water.

First drain the water from the system (▷), then use your bleed-valve key to unscrew the old valve completely out of the blanking plug (**1**). Wind some PTFE tape (▷) round the threads of the automatic valve (**2**) and screw it finger tight into the blanking plug (**3**). Refill the system (▷) and if any water appears round the threads of the new valve tighten it further with a spanner (**4**).

If, when the system is going again, the radiator still feels cool on top it may be that a larger amount of air has collected than the bleed valve can cope with. In this case switch off the pump and unscrew the valve until you hear air hissing out. Tighten it again when the hissing stops and the first trickle of water appears, then restart the pump.

 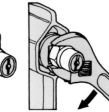

1 Unscrew old valve   **2 Tape the new one**   **3 Screw it finger tight**   **4 Stop any leak in use**

HOW TO REMOVE A RADIATOR

You can remove an individual radiator while the wall behind it is decorated without having to drain the whole system. You simply close the valves at the ends of the radiator, drain it and then remove it.

Shut off both valves, turning the shank of the lockshield valve clockwise with a key or an adjustable spanner (**1**). Note the number of turns needed to close it so that later you can reopen it by the same amount.

Make sure that you have plenty of rag for mopping up spillage, also a jug and a large bowl. As the water in the radiator will be very dirty you should also roll back the floor covering before you start if possible.

Unscrew the cap-nut that holds one of the valves to the adaptor in the end of the radiator (**2**). Hold the jug under the joint and open the bleed valve slowly (**3**) to let the water drain out. Transfer the water from jug to bowl and keep going until no more can be drained.

Unscrew the cap-nut that holds the other valve onto the radiator, lift the radiator free from its wall brackets (**4**) and drain any remaining water into the bowl. Unscrew the wall brackets to decorate.

To replace the radiator after decorating screw the brackets back in place, hang the radiator on them and tighten the cap-nuts on both valves. Close the bleed valve and open both radiator valves, the lockshield valve by the same number of turns as you used to close it. Finally use the bleed valve to release any trapped air.

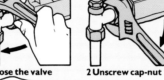

1 Close the valve   **2 Unscrew cap-nut**

3 Open bleed valve

4 Final draining
Lift radiator from brackets and drain off any remaining water.

RADIATOR VALVES

VALVE HEAD

GLAND NUT

**Tightening
gland nut**
Tighten the gland nut
with a spanner to stop
a leak from a radiator
valve spindle. If the
leak persists, replace
the valve (See right).

Curing a leaking radiator valve

If a manual-control valve or lockshield valve on a radiator seems to be leaking it's most likely that one of the cap-nuts that secure it to the water pipe and to the radiator's valve adaptor needs some tightening up.

Tighten the suspect cap-nut with an adjustable spanner while you hold the body of the valve with a pipe wrench to prevent it moving. If this doesn't work the valve will have to be replaced.

If the leak seems to be from the valve adaptor in the radiator the joint will have to be remade in the same way as when a new valve is fitted (See below). If the leak seems to be from the valve spindle tighten the gland nut (See left) or replace the valve.

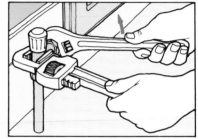
Grip leaky valve with wrench to tighten cap-nut

Replacing a worn or damaged valve

Be sure that the new valve is exactly like the old one, or it may not align with the water pipe. Drain the heating system (◁) and lay rags under the valve to catch any remaining dregs that may come out of the radiator.

Hold the body of the valve with a wrench and use an adjustable spanner to unscrew the cap-nuts that hold the valve to the water pipe and to the adaptor in the end of the radiator (**1**). Lift the valve from the end of the pipe (**2**). If the valve being replaced is a lockshield valve don't remove it before you have closed it, counting the number of turns needed so that you can open the new valve by the same number to balance the radiator.

Unscrew the adaptor from the radiator (**3**). You may manage this with an adjustable spanner or you may need a special hexagonal radiator spanner, depending on the type of adaptor.

Fitting the new one

Ensure that the threads in the end of the radiator are clean and wind PTFE tape (◁) four or five times round the thread of the new valve's adaptor, then screw it into the end of the radiator by hand and tighten it a further 1½ turns with the spanner.

Slide the valve cap-nut and a new olive over the end of the water pipe and fit the valve to the end of the pipe (**4**), but don't tighten the cap-nut at this stage. First align the valve body with the adaptor and tighten the cap-nut that holds them together (**5**). Hold the valve body firm with a wrench while you do this. Now tighten the cap-nut that holds the valve to the water pipe (**6**).

Finally refill the system, check for leaks at the joints of the new valves and tighten the cap-nuts some more if that seems necessary.

DEALING WITH A JAMMED OLIVE

If the olive is jammed onto the pipe, cut the pipe off below floorboard level and make up a new section. Join it to the old pipe by means of either a capillary or a compression joint.

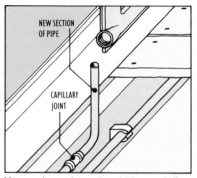
NEW SECTION OF PIPE

CAPILLARY JOINT

New section replaces pipe with jammed olive

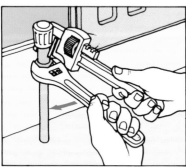
1 Hold the valve firm and loosen both cap-nuts

2 Unscrew the cap-nuts and lift the valve out

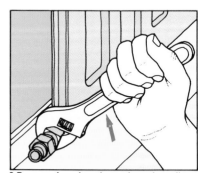
3 Remove the valve adaptor from the radiator

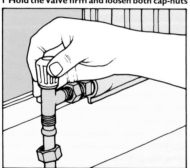
4 Fit new adaptor, then fit new valve to pipe

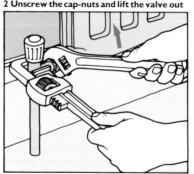
5 Connect valve to adaptor and tighten cap-nut

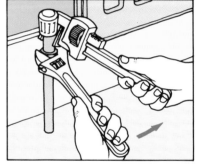
6 Tighten cap-nut holding valve to water pipe

REPLACING A CORRODED OR DAMAGED RADIATOR

Try to obtain a new radiator of exactly the same model as the one you wish to replace. This will make the job easier.

Simple replacement

Drain and remove the old radiator (▷). With it clear of the wall unscrew the valve adaptors from the bottom with an adjustable spanner or, if necessary, a hexagonal radiator spanner. Unscrew the bleed valve with its key, and then the two blanking plugs from the top of the radiator, using a square or hexagonal radiator spanner **(1)**.

With wire wool clean up the threads of both adaptors and both blanking plugs **(2)**, then wind four or five turns of PTFE tape (▷) round the threads **(3)**. Screw them into the new radiator and the bleed valve into the blanking plug.

Hang the new radiator on its wall brackets and connect the valves to their adaptors. Open the valves and fill and bleed the radiators (▷).

Replacement with a different pattern radiator

Rather more work is involved in the replacement if you can't get a radiator of the same pattern as the old one. You'll have to fit new wall brackets and alter the water pipes.

Drain the system (▷), then take the old brackets off the wall. Lay the new radiator face down on the floor and slide one of its brackets onto the hangers welded to the back of the radiator. Measure from the top of the bracket to the bottom of the radiator, add 100 or 125mm (4 or 5in) for clearance under the radiator, then mark a horizontal line on the wall that distance from the floor. Now measure the distance between the centres of the radiator hangers and make two marks on the horizontal line that distance apart and at equal distances from the two water pipes **(1)**.

Line up the brackets with the pencil marks, mark their fixing screw holes, drill and plug the holes and fix the brackets in place **(2)**.

Lift up the floorboards below the radiator's position and cut off the vertical portions of the feed and return pipes. Connect the valves to the radiator and hang it on its brackets. Slip a short length of pipe into each valve as a guide for any further trimming of the pipes under the floor. Connect these lengths to the original pipes **(3)** with capillary or compression fittings (▷), then connect the new pipes to the valves (▷). Refill the system and check the connections and joints for leaks.

1 Removing the plug
Use a radiator spanner to unscrew the blanking plug at each end of the radiator.

2 Cleaning the threads
Use wire wool to clean any corrosion from the threads of both blanking plugs and valve adaptors.

3 Taping the threads
Make the threaded joints watertight by wrapping PTFE tape several times around each component before screwing them into the new radiator.

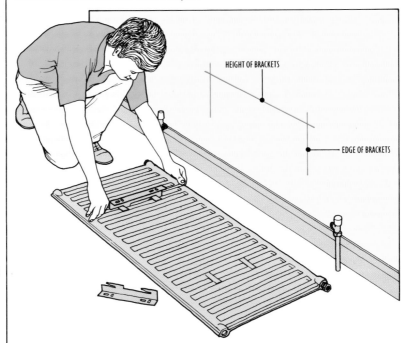

HEIGHT OF BRACKETS

EDGE OF BRACKETS

1 Taking the measurements
Measure the positions of the radiator brackets and transfer the measurements to the wall. Double-check the results to make sure the radiator is equidistant between the two pipes projecting from the floor.

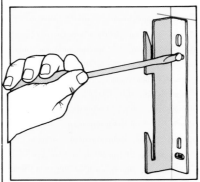

2 Securing the brackets
Screw the mounting brackets to the wall
Make sure they are on the right side of the line.

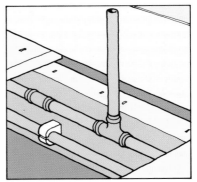

3 Connecting up
Connect the new section of pipework
The vertical pipe aligns with the radiator valve.

CIRCULATING PUMPS

Wet central heating depends on a steady cycle of hot water from boiler to radiators and back to the boiler for reheating. This is the pump's job. A faulty pump means poor circulation. A failed pump means none.

Bleeding the pump

If your radiators don't seem to be warming up, though you can hear or feel the pump running, it's likely that an airlock has formed in the pump and its impeller is spinning in air. The air must be bled from the pump, a job that's done in the same way as bleeding a radiator. You'll find a screw-in valve for the purpose in the pump's outer casing.

The valve's position varies with the different makes but it is usually marked.

Switch off the pump, have a jug or jam jar handy to catch any water spillage and open the valve with a screwdriver or vent key. Open it only slightly, until you hear air hissing out. When the hissing stops and a drop of water appears close the valve fully.

Open the bleed valve with a screwdriver

Adjusting the pump

Central heating pumps are of two kinds: fixed head and variable head. Fixed-head units run at a single speed, forcing the water round the system at a fixed rate. Variable-head pumps can be adjusted to run at different speeds, circulating the water at different rates.

When a variable-head pump is fitted as part of a central heating system the installer adjusts its speed after balancing all the radiators so that each room reaches its 'design temperature'. If you find that your rooms are not as warm as you would like, though you have opened the manual radiator valves fully, you can adjust the pump speed. But first check that all radiators show the same temperature drop between their inlets and outlets. You can get clip-on thermometers for the job from a

plumbers' merchant. You will need a pair of them.

Clip one thermometer to the feed pipe just below the radiator valve and the other to the return pipe below its valve (**1**). The difference between the temperatures registered by the two should be about 7°C (20°F). If it is not, uncover the lockshield valve and close it further (to increase the difference) or open it more (to reduce the difference).

Having balanced the radiators you can now adjust the pump. Switch it off and then turn the speed adjustment up (**2**), one step at a time, until you are getting the overall temperatures you want. You may be able to work the adjustment by hand or you may need some special tool, such as an Allen key, depending on the make and model of your pump.

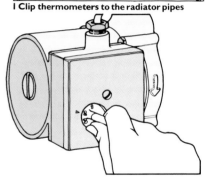

1 Clip thermometers to the radiator pipes

2 Adjust pump speed to increase temperature

Replacing a worn pump

If you have to replace your circulating pump be quite sure that the one you buy is of exactly the same make and model as the old one, or seek the advice of a professional installer.

Turn off the boiler and close the isolating valves on each side of the pump. If there are no isolating valves you will have to drain down the whole system (◁).

Identify the electrical circuit that controls the pump and remove the fuse of that circuit from the consumer unit (◁), then take the cover plate off the pump and disconnect its wiring (**1**).

Have a bowl or bucket at hand to catch any water left in the pump, also some old rags for any mopping up that you may have to do. Undo the nuts that hold the pump to the valves or the pipework with an adjustable spanner (**2**) and catch the water as it flows out.

Remove the pump and fit the new one in its place, taking care to fit correctly any sealing washers that are provided (**3**), then tighten up the retaining nuts.

Take the cover plate off the new pump, feed in the flex, connect the wires to the pump's terminals (**4**) and replace the cover plate. If the pump is of the variable-head type (See above) set the speed control to the speed indicated on the old pump.

Open both isolating valves – or if the system has been drained refill it (◁) – check the pump connections for leaks and tighten them if necessary, then open the pump's bleed valve to release any air that may have become trapped in it. Finally replace the fuse in the consumer unit and test the pump.

1 Remove cover plate   2 Undo connecting nuts

3 Attach new pump   4 Connect power flex

CONTROL VALVES

The control valves are vital to the effective working of a modern central heating system, for it is through them that the various timers and thermostats are able to adjust the levels of heating precisely to the programmed requirements of the householder.

Worn or faulty control valves can seriously affect the reliability of the system and should be replaced promptly.

Replacing a faulty valve

First ensure that the replacement valve that you buy is of exactly the same pattern as the faulty one, or seek professional advice.

Drain down the system (▷), then identify the electrical circuit that services the central heating controls and take its fuse out of the consumer unit.

The electric flex from the valve will be connected to the terminals of a nearby junction box, which will also be linked to the heating system's other controls. Take the cover off the junction box and disconnect the wiring for the valve. As you do this you should carefully note the connections so as to make reconnection easier.

You will probably not be able to take the old valve out of the pipe run by simply unscrewing its cap-nuts, as you won't be able to pull the ends of the pipe free of their sockets in the valve. Instead cut through the pipe on each side of the valve (**1**) and take out the section, complete with valve, then make up two pieces of pipe to fit on either side of the new control valve.

Assemble the valve with its olives and cap-nuts, pipes and joints, but only loosely at first, and fit the assembly into the pipe run (**2**).

There should be enough play in the joints to allow the assembly to be sprung into place, and this may be helped if the original pipes on each side of the valve position are first freed from their clips.

When the pipes and valve are in place connect them to the original pipework with compression or capillary joints (▷), then tighten the valve cap-nuts. Hold the body of the valve with a second spanner to prevent it turning (**3**).

Reconnect the flex to the terminals of the junction box and replace its cover plate, then replace the fuse in the consumer unit.

Refill the heating system and check the working of the valve by adjusting the timer or thermostat that controls it.

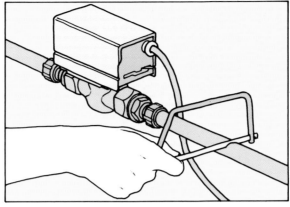

1 Removing the valve
If you cannot disconnect the valve, cut through the pipe on each side of it with a hacksaw.

SEE ALSO

Details for: ▷	
Pipe joints	21-22
Draining system	55
Heating controls	53

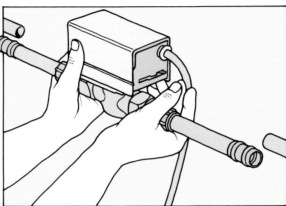

2 Fitting new valve
With the new valve connected to short sections of pipe, spring the assembly into the pipe run.

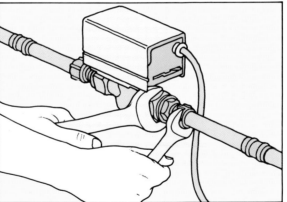

3 Closing the joints
Having connected the pipework, tighten the valve cap-nuts on each side with a pair of spanners.

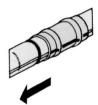

Slip coupling
If you cannot spring pipework to locate a conventional soldered joint (▷) use a slip coupling which is free to slide along the pipe to cover the junction.

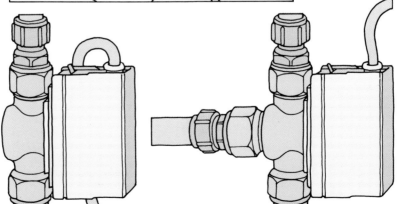

Far left
Two-port control valve
A two-port valve seals off a section of pipework when water within that section has reached the required temperature.

Left
Three-port control valve
This type of valve can independently isolate central heating or hot water circuits.

61

GUTTERING

Guttering collects the rainwater that runs down a roof and leads it to a downpipe through which it discharges into a drain. Good rainwater disposal is vital in preventing damp developing in the fabric of a house.

SEE ALSO

◁ Details for:
Fitting guttering   64

Roof drainage

The size and layout of a roof drainage system should enable it to discharge all the water from a given roof area. The flow load determining the guttering's capacity depends mainly on the area of the roof. Makers of rainwater goods usually specify the maximum area for a given size and profile of gutter based on a rainfall rate of 75mm/hr (3in/hr). If you replace an old gutter, perished but of the right capacity, have the size that of the original or slightly larger.

A downpipe's position can affect the system's performance. A system with a central downpipe can serve double the roof area of one with an end outlet. A right-angled bend will reduce the flow capacity by about 20 per cent if it is near the outlet.

In practice, unless you are working on a new building, the positions of drains and downpipes are already fixed.

Sizes
Gutter sizes are generally specified by their overall width in cross section and sometimes by their depth as well.

TYPICAL PROFILES AND SIZES OF GUTTERING

Half round	Ogee (OG)	Moulded OG	Box
75mm (3in)			
100mm (4in)	100mm (4in)	100 x 75mm (4 x 3in)	100 x 75mm (4 x 3in)
112mm (4½in)	112mm (4½in)		
125mm (5in)	125mm (5in)	125 x 100mm (5 x 4in)	125 x 100mm (5 x 4in)
150mm (6in)	150 x 100mm (6 x 4in)	150 x 100mm (6 x 4in)	

TYPES OF GUTTERING

The guttering on domestic buildings is used in various ways adapted to the design of the roof.

EAVES GUTTERS

The commonest types by far are the eaves gutters, which are fixed along the eaves fascia boards (See below). They are made in many materials and designs.

PARAPET GUTTERS

Parapet gutters are generally found in older houses and may serve a flat or pitched roof set between two parapet walls. This type is generally purpose-made as part of the original structure of the roof and is usually covered with a metal or bituminous roofing material.

VALLEY GUTTERS

Valley gutters are a form of flashing used at the junctions between sloping roofs. They are not gutter systems in themselves but they direct the rainwater into eaves or parapet gutters.

EAVES GUTTER SYSTEMS

Eaves gutter systems are fabricated in cast iron, cast and rolled sheet aluminium, asbestos cement and a uPVC rigid plastic. With the exception of the roll-formed aluminium type the systems are made up from basic lengths of gutter and downpipes with a range of fittings (See diagram).

Moulded or cast gutters have a socket at one end into which the plain spigot end of the next section is jointed.

For gutters that are not symmetrical in section, such as an OG, this means that components are left- or right-handed, and this has to be noted when replacement parts are being ordered.

Traditional cast iron and modern aluminium guttering may be compatible should you wish to renew only a part of your system, or extend it, but with the modern patented-design plastic systems you will have to stay with the same make for, though similar in style, they are not interchangeable.

1 Stopend
Internal and external fittings for socketed or non-socketed types.

2 Gutter brackets
Normally screwed to fascia board, but some can fix to rafter bracket arms.

3 Guttering
In various profiles and lengths of 1.8 to 3m (6 to 10ft) with socket at one end or spigots both ends.

4 Downpipe
Available in 1.8 to 3m (6 to 10ft) lengths. Metal types may have integral fixing lugs.

5 Hopperhead
May be used as part of downpipe system to receive waste pipes from another source.

6 Pipe clip
Secures downpipes to wall.

7 Running outlet
May be double or single socketed.

8 Gutter angle
Available in 90, 120 and 135 degree angles in most systems for turning corners.

9 Stopend outlet
Used with downpipe at an end.

10 Offset
Used on guttering fitted to overhanging eaves. Available in standard projections or can be made up with special offset bends and a length of downpipe.

11 Shoe
Throws water clear of a wall into open gulley (◁).

Profiles
A diverse range of profiles is available, some based on classic profiles, others of modern form. See chart above, for typical sizes.

Plain half round

Ogee (OG)

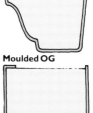

Moulded OG

Box

MAINTENANCE

Cast iron, cast aluminium and asbestos cement guttering are all rigid and will support a ladder. But this is not really advisable, and it is much better to use a ladder stay (▷). Never prop a ladder against either plastic or roll-formed aluminium gutters.

Inspect and clean out the interiors of gutters regularly. Gutters concentrate the dirt, and sometimes sand washed down from the tiles by the rain. This can quickly build up if the flow of water is restricted by leaves or twigs. Birds' nests also can effectively block the guttering or downpipes.

The weight of standing water can distort plastic guttering, and if a blockage that is causing the gutter to overflow is left unchecked it can lead to problems with damp in the walls.

Removing debris
First block the gutter outlet with rag. With a shaped piece of plastic laminate scrape the silt into a heap, scoop it out of the gutter with a garden trowel and deposit it in a bucket hung from the ladder. Sweep the gutter clean with a stiff hand brush.

Remove the rag and flush the gutter down with a bucket of water.

Fit a wire or plastic 'balloon' to prevent debris falling into the downpipe or birds nesting on top of it.

Snow and ice
Plastic guttering can be badly distorted and even broken by snow and ice building up in it. Dislodge the build-up with a broom from an upstairs window if you can reach it safely. Otherwise climb a ladder to remove it.

If snow and ice become a regular seasonal problem you should screw a snow board made from 75 x 25mm (3 x 1in) planed softwood treated with a wood preservative and painted. Fix it to stand about 25mm (1in) above the eaves tiles, using 25 x 6mm (1 x ¼in) steel straps bent as required.

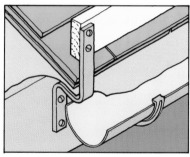
A snow board protects gutters or glazed roofs

GUTTERING MATERIALS

CAST IRON

The cast iron rainwater systems common on old houses are mostly of the OG type, fixed to the fascia board by mushroom-headed short screws through the back of the gutter above the water line and spaced about 600mm (2ft) apart.

Each 1.8m (6ft) standard length of the guttering has a socket end into which the plain spigot end of the next piece fits **(1)**. Short bolts secure the joint and a bedding of putty forms a seal when they are tightened **(2)**.

Cast iron is heavy and brittle, and installing or dismantling such a system needs two people. The iron can be cut with a hacksaw and drilled with standard twist drills in a power tool.

The guttering needs normal regular painting, and a bituminous paint applied inside makes for a longer life. If it is unprotected it will rust, usually along the back edge round the screws. Badly rusted guttering should be replaced, as it is likely to collapse.

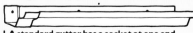
1 A standard gutter has a socket at one end

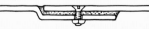
2 The joint is sealed with putty then bolted

CAST ALUMINIUM

Cast aluminium guttering comes in a wide range of profiles, including OG, moulded OG and half round. It is assembled in a similar way to cast iron guttering, with bolted joints, but a flexible mastic is used instead of putty to make the seals. The guttering may be fitted to the fascia with screws through the back, or with gutter brackets. All of the fixings should also be of aluminium.

Cast aluminium is about one third the weight of cast iron and can be left unpainted, but in some situations it can corrode, and if it is used as part of a cast iron system all the aluminium surfaces must be protected with zinc chromate or bituminous paint. It can be worked with ordinary metal-working tools.

ASBESTOS CEMENT

Asbestos cement guttering is of the socket-and-spigot type. The joints are secured with galvanised iron bolts and the seals are made with a mastic jointing compound. The guttering is produced in half round profiles in a range of several sizes. It is fixed to the house fascia board with gutter brackets, and these should not be spaced more than 900m (3ft) apart.

Asbestos cement has good weathering properties and does not need to be painted. It can be cut with a hacksaw and drilled normally (▷).

ROLLED SHEET ALUMINIUM

Rolled sheet aluminium guttering is a moulded lightweight OG system made from thin, prepainted flat sheet aluminium which is roll-formed to the gutter shape by a portable machine. This is done on site by the suppliers, and unbroken lengths are made to measure.

The end stops and angles are supplied as separate items, crimped to the ends of the gutter sections. Outlets are formed by punching holes in the bottom.

Simple metal fixing brackets are clipped to the front and back edges of the guttering and fixed to the fascia with drive screws. The system needs no maintenance but can be painted.

UPVC

Guttering of unplasticised PVC (uPVC) is now the most widely used, for new buildings and for replacing old systems. In many profiles and sizes, it is self-coloured in brown, black, grey and white. It needs no painting.

Most uPVC systems use clip-fastened joints with synthetic rubber gaskets to form the seals. Some use a solvent cement to weld the joints. Downpipes may be a push fit, and sealed with an 'O' ring or solvent-welded. The guttering is usually supported by brackets, but some systems use screws in the back edge of the outlet and corner fittings for easier installation.

SEE ALSO

Details for: ▷	
Ladder stay	77
Cutting asbestos	72

Cast iron OG gutter

Cast aluminium

RAFTER BRACKET   FASCIA BRACKET

Gutter brackets

DRIVE SCREW

Sheet aluminium

FASCIA BRACKET

Plastic guttering

FITTING NEW GUTTERING AND DOWNPIPE

When your old gutter system reaches the end of its useful life you should replace it. Try to do so with a system in the same style or, at least, one that goes with the character of your house. If you plan to install the guttering yourself a plastic system is probably the best choice, being easy to handle.

SEE ALSO
◁ Details for:
Hacksaw   72-73

Installing the guttering

Measure round the base of the house to find the total length of gutter needed, and note the number and type of fittings to be ordered.

Use a plumb line to mark the position of the gutter outlet – directly over the existing drain – on the fascia board **(1)** . Screw the outlet or its support bracket – depending on the system – to the fascia no more than 50mm (2in) below the tile level **(2)** .

Fix a gutter bracket at the opposite end of the run, close to the top of the fascia board. This is to give a fall of at least 25mm (1in) in 15m (50ft) **(3)** . Run a taut string between the bracket and outlet and fix the rest of the brackets along the slope of the string, spaced no more than 1m (3ft 3in) apart **(4)** . There should be a bracket at every joint unless the system uses screw-fixed outlets and angles **(5)** .

Fitting the gutter

Tuck the back edge of a length of gutter under the roofing felt and into the rear lips of the brackets, then clip its front edge into all of the brackets **(6)** .

Fit the second length in the same way, with its spigot end pushed into the socket of the first length. Some pressure will be needed to compress the rubber seal. Leave a gap of about 6mm (1/4in) between the end of the spigot and the shoulder of the socket to allow for expansion.

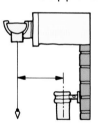

6 Clip the guttering into the brackets

7 Use an adaptor to join different systems

Cutting the gutter
Cut the gutter squarely with a hacksaw. You can snap a clip or bracket over it first to give rigidity and guide the cut. Smooth the rough edges with a file. In some systems notches for the clips are made in the gutter's front and back edges; this can be done with a file.

Connecting to existing guttering
To renew guttering on a terrace house may mean joining your system to your neighbours'. There are left- and right-hand adaptors for this.

Remove your old guttering to the nearest joint between the houses, bolt the adaptor on, sealing the joint with mastic, and fix the new plastic gutter with the clip provided. **(7)** .

Fitting the downpipe

Work downward from the gutter outlet. If the eaves overhang you will need to fit an offset.

Fit a clip to the top of a length of downpipe. Hold it against the wall and measure the distance from its centre to a plumb line dropped through the outlet's centre **(8)** . You may find an offset to fit but will most likely have to make it up with offset bends and pipe. Use a solvent cement and assemble it on a table so that the bends lie in the same plane.

Fit the offset to the outlet spigot and the pipe to the offset. Adjust the pipe so that the clip's back plate falls on a mortar joint **(9)** . Trim the offset spigot if necessary.

Mark the fixings, drill and plug the wall and fix the pipe and clip with plated round-head screws.

Mark and fix the lower lengths of pipe in the same way, with a 6mm (1/4in) expansion gap between each pipe and the socket shoulder. Fit extra clips at the centre of any pipe longer than 2m (6ft 6in).

Cut the bottom pipe to length and fit a shoe in the same way **(10)** . If the pipe is jointed into a gulley trap **(11)** or a drainsocket you may have to work from the bottom.

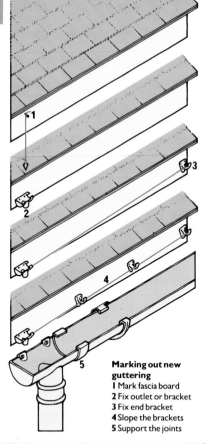

Marking out new guttering
1 Mark fascia board
2 Fix outlet or bracket
3 Fix end bracket
4 Slope the brackets
5 Support the joints

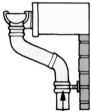 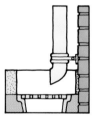

8 Drop a plumb line   **9 Fit an offset**   **10 Finish with a shoe**   **11 Fit into gulley**

REPAIRING GUTTERS AND DOWNPIPES

It is always better to replace a damaged part of a gutter system than to repair it, but a neat repair that stays watertight can be regarded as permanent.

Mending a crack
Chipped or cracked guttering and downpipes of cast iron or asbestos cement can be repaired with a 'cement bandage'.

Clean the surface, cut the bandage to length and soak it in water for 15 to 20 seconds. Wearing rubber gloves position the bandage over the crack, smooth it in place and leave it to set hard. If possible cover it with polythene for 72 hours to delay the drying time.

Using epoxy putty
You can build up the chipped edge of a cast iron gutter with epoxy putty. Tape a waxed or polythene-lined piece of card across the outside of the broken edge and bent to follow the contour of the gutter. Mix the two-part putty, fill the gap with it and remove the cardboard 'former' when the putty sets.

Insulating a hot water cylinder

Many people think that an uninsulated cylinder is providing a useful source of heat in an airing cupboard, but in fact it squanders a surprising amount of energy. Even a lagged cylinder should provide ample background heat in an enclosed cupboard – but if not, an uninsulated pipe will.

Proprietary cylinder jackets are made from segments of 80 to 100mm (3¼ to 4in) thick mineral-fibre insulation material wrapped in plastic. Measure the approximate height and circumference of the cylinder to choose the right size. If necessary, buy a larger jacket rather than one that is too small. Make sure you buy a good-quality jacket by checking that it is marked with the British Standard kite mark (BS 5615).

If you should ever have to replace the cylinder, consider buying a pre-insulated version, of which there are various types on the market (▷).

Thread the tapered ends of the jacket segments onto a length of string and tie it round the pipe at the top of the cylinder. Distribute the segments evenly around the cylinder and wrap the straps or string provided around it to hold the insulation in place.

Spread out the segments to make sure the edges are butted together and tuck the insulation around the pipes and the cylinder thermostat.

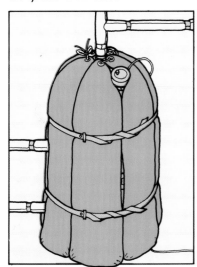

Lagging a hot water cylinder
Fit a jacket snugly around the cylinder and wrap insulating foam tubes (See above right) around the pipework, especially the vent pipe directly above the cylinder.

Lagging pipe runs

You should insulate hot water pipes where their radiant heat is not contributing to the warmth of your home, and also cold water pipe runs in unheated areas of the house, where they could freeze. You can wrap pipework in one of several lagging bandages, some of which are self-adhesive, but it is more convenient to use foamed plastic tubes designed for the purpose, especially along pipes running close and clipped to a wall, which would be awkward to wrap.

Plastic tubes are made to fit pipes of different diameters and the tube walls vary in thickness from 10mm to 20mm (½in to ¾in). More expensive tubing incorporates a metallic foil backing to reflect some of the heat back into hot water pipes.

Most tubes are pre-slit along their length so that they can be sprung over the pipe (**1**). Butt successive lengths of tube end-to-end and seal the joints with PVC adhesive tape.

At a bend, cut small segments out of the split edge so it bends without crimping. Fit it around the pipe (**2**) and seal the closed joints with tape. If pipe is joined with an elbow fitting (▷), mitre the ends of the two lengths of tube, butt them together (**3**) and seal with tape.

Cut lengths of tube to fit completely around a tee-joint, linking them with a wedge-shaped butt joint (**4**) and seal with tape as before.

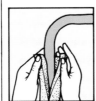

| 1 Spring onto pipe | 2 Cut to fit bend | 3 Mitre over elbows | 4 Butt at tee-joint |

SEE ALSO	
Details for: ▷	
Plumbing joints	20
Cylinders	48
Radiator roller	77

Reflecting heat from a radiator

Up to 25 per cent of the radiant heat from a radiator on an outside wall is lost to the wall behind. Reclaim perhaps half this wasted heat by installing a foil-faced, expanded polystyrene lining behind the radiator to reflect it back into the room.

The material is available as rolls, sheets or tiles to fit any size and shape of radiator. It is easier to stick the foil on the wall when the radiator is removed for decorating but it is not an essential requirement.

Turn off the radiator and measure it, including the position of the brackets. Use a sharp trimming knife or scissors to cut the foil to size so that it is slightly smaller than the radiator all round. Cut narrow slots to fit over the fixing brackets (**1**).

Apply heavy-duty fungicidal wallpaper paste to the back of the sheet and slide it behind the radiator (**2**). Rub it down with a radiator roller (▷) or smooth it against the wall with a wooden batten. Allow enough time for the adhesive to dry before turning the radiator on again.

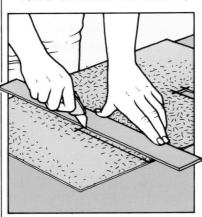

1 Cut slots to align with wall brackets

2 Slide lining behind radiator and press to wall

ESSENTIAL ELECTRICS

It is important to have a basic knowledge of electrics in order to install certain kitchen and bathroom appliances. You are also required to connect metal plumbing to earth to comply with official Wiring Regulations. If you are in any doubt concerning procedures for safe wiring, consult an electrician registered with the National Inspection Council for Electrical Installation Contracting.

● **PME**
Some districts, especially in country areas, are provided with an earthing system called 'protective multiple earth' (PME). Earth-leakage current is fed back to the Electricity Board substation along the neutral return wire, and so to earth. If you have this system (check with the Electricity Board), hire an electrician for any but the most minor type of work.

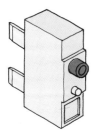

Miniature circuit breakers
Some consumer units are fitted with MCBs instead of fuses. You operate a switch or a button to 'off' to isolate a particular circuit. When a fault occurs, the MCB switches off automatically.

The sealing chamber

The main cable terminates at the service head, or sealing chamber, which contains the service fuse. This fuse prevents the neighbourhood being affected if there should be a serious fault in your circuitry. A cable connects the sealing chamber to the meter, which registers how much power is used. The meter and sealing chamber belong to the Electricity Board and must not be tampered with. The meter is sealed to detect interference.

If you use the cheap night-time power for storage heaters and hot water a time switch will be mounted somewhere between the sealing chamber and the meter.

Consumer units

Electricity is fed to and from the consumer unit by 'meter leads', thick single-core cables made up of several wires twisted together. The consumer unit is a box that contains the fuseways which protect the individual circuits in the house. It also incorporates the main isolating switch with which you can cut off the supply of power to the whole of the house.

In a house where several new circuits have been installed over the years the number of circuits may exceed the number of fuseways in the consumer unit, so an individual switchfuse unit – or more than one – may have to be mounted alongside the main unit. Switchfuse units comprise a single fuseway and an isolating switch. They too are connected to the meter by means of meter leads.

If your home is heated by storage heaters you will probably have a separate consumer unit for the circuits that supply the heaters.

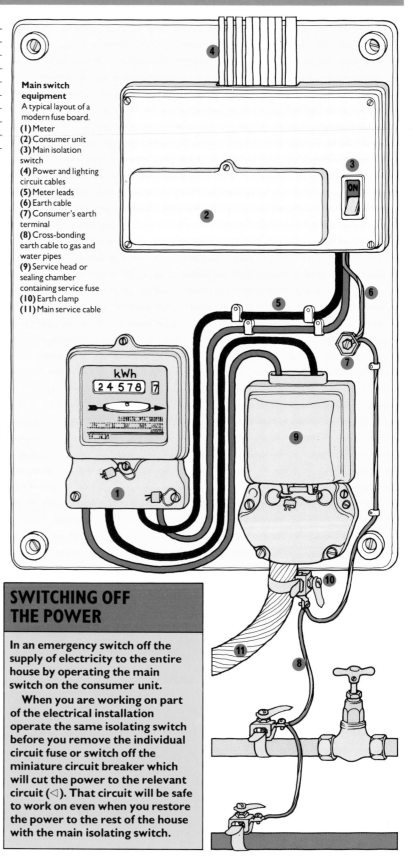

Main switch equipment
A typical layout of a modern fuse board.
(**1**) Meter
(**2**) Consumer unit
(**3**) Main isolation switch
(**4**) Power and lighting circuit cables
(**5**) Meter leads
(**6**) Earth cable
(**7**) Consumer's earth terminal
(**8**) Cross-bonding earth cable to gas and water pipes
(**9**) Service head or sealing chamber containing service fuse
(**10**) Earth clamp
(**11**) Main service cable

SWITCHING OFF THE POWER

In an emergency switch off the supply of electricity to the entire house by operating the main switch on the consumer unit.

When you are working on part of the electrical installation operate the same isolating switch before you remove the individual circuit fuse or switch off the miniature circuit breaker which will cut the power to the relevant circuit (◁). That circuit will be safe to work on even when you restore the power to the rest of the house with the main isolating switch.

DEALING WITH ELECTRIC SHOCK

If someone in your presence gets an electric shock and is still in contact with its source, turn off the current at once by pulling out the plug or switching off at the socket or the consumer unit. If you cannot do this don't take hold of the person; the current may pass through you too. Pull the victim free with a dry towel, a necktie or something like that, or knock their hand free of the electrical equipment with a piece of wood. As a last resort free the victim, using their loose clothing, but without touching the body.

Don't try to move anyone who has fallen as a result of electric shock. They may have sustained other injuries. Wrap them in a blanket or coat to keep warm until they can move themselves.

Treat electrical burns by reducing the heat of the injury under slowly running cold water once the person can move and is no longer in contact with the electrical equipment. Then apply a dry dressing and seek medical advice.

Isolating the victim
If a person sustains an electric shock turn off the supply of electricity immediately, either at the consumer unit or at a socket (1). If this is not possible, pull the victim free with a dry towel, or knock their hand free of the electrical equipment (2) with a piece of wood or a broom.

ARTIFICIAL RESPIRATION

Severe electric shock can make a person stop breathing. Having freed them from the electricity supply, revive them by means of artificial respiration.

Clear the airways
Clear the victim's airways by loosening the clothing round the neck, chest and waist. Make sure that the mouth is free of food and remove any dentures (1). Lay the person on his or her back and tilt the head back while supporting the back of the neck with one hand.

l **Clear the mouth of food or dentures**

Restart the breathing
With your free hand close and open the jaw several times in an attempt to restart the person's breathing (2). If this does not succeed quickly, try more direct methods of artificial respiration.

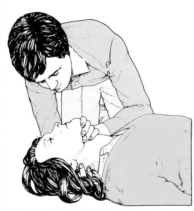

2 **Open and close victim's jaw several times**

Mouth to nose
Cover the victim's mouth with one hand and blow firmly into the nose (3). Look for signs of the chest rising and falling, then blow again three or four times in rapid succession. Repeat this procedure every four or five seconds until normal breathing resumes.

Mouth to mouth
Pinch shut the victim's nostrils, then cover the mouth with your own, making a seal all round (4), and proceed as in mouth to nose above.

3 **Mouth to nose**   4 **Mouth to mouth**

Reviving a child
With a baby or small child cover both the nose and the mouth at the same time with your own mouth (5), then proceed as above.

5 **Cover a baby's nose and mouth**

Recovery
Once breathing has started again, turn the victim face down with the head turned sideways and tilted up slightly so that the chin juts out. This will keep the airways open.

Lift one arm and one leg out from the body (6), then with blankets or coats arrange for the victim to stay warm while you summon medical help.

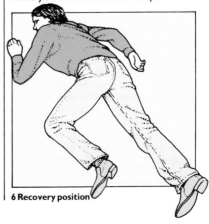

6 **Recovery position**

SEE ALSO
Details for: ▷
Safety tips   68

BATHROOM SAFETY

● **Supplementary bonding in a kitchen**
Supplementary bonding regulations apply to kitchens as well as bathrooms. Bond metal sink units, metallic supply and wastepipes, radiators and central heating pipework. Space and water heaters must be bonded as for bathrooms.

Water and electricity form a very dangerous combination, for water is a highly efficient conductor of electric current. For this reason bathrooms are potentially the most dangerous areas in terms of electricity. Where there are so many exposed pipes and fittings, combined with wet conditions, stringent regulations must be observed if fatal accidents are to be avoided.

GENERAL SAFETY

● No sockets should be fitted in a bathroom except special ones approved for electric shavers (◁).

● Regulations stipulate that any standard light switches in bathrooms must be out of reach of anyone using a shower, bath or washbasin. The only sure way of complying with this is to fit nothing but ceiling-mounted pull-cord switches.

● Any bathroom heater must comply with IEE Regulations (◁).

● If you have a shower unit in a bedroom it must be at least 2.5m (8ft) from any socket outlet.

● Light fittings must also be out of reach, so fit a close-mounted ceiling light, properly enclosed, rather than a pendant fitting.

● Never use portable fires or other appliances such as hair dryers in a bathroom even if they are plugged into a socket outside.

WARNING

Have supplementary bonding tested by a qualified electrician. If you have had no previous experience of wiring and making connections have supplementary bonding installed by a professional.

Supplementary bonding

In a bathroom there are many non-electrical metallic components such as metal baths and basins, supply pipes to bath and basin taps, metal wastepipes, radiators, central heating pipework and so on, all of which could become dangerous if they were to come into contact with a live electrical conductor. To ensure that such an occurrence would blow a fuse in the consumer unit, Wiring Regulations specify that all these metal components must be connected one to another by an earth conductor which itself is connected to a terminal on the earthing block in the consumer unit. This is known as supplementary bonding and is required for new bathrooms even when there is no electrical equipment installed in the room and even though the water and gas pipes are bonded to the consumer's earth terminal near the consumer unit (◁). When electrical equipment like a heater or shower is fitted in a bathroom, that too must be supplementary bonded by connecting its metalwork, such as the casing, to the non-electrical pipework even though the appliance is connected to the earthing conductor in the supply cable.

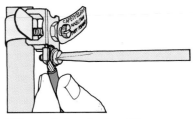

Supplementary bonding in a bathroom

Making the connections

Wiring Regulations specify the minimum size of earthing conductor that can be used for supplementary bonding in different situations so that large electrical installations can be costed economically. In a home environment use $6mm^2$ single-core cable insulated with green or green/yellow PVC for all the supplementary bonding. It is large enough to be safe in any domestic situation unless your house is wired with Protective Multiple Earthing (◁) in which case you should consult a professional. For a neat appearance plan the route of the earth cable to run from point to point behind the bath panel, under floorboards and through basin pedestals. If necessary run the cable through a hollow wall or under plaster like any other electrical cable.

Connecting to pipework

Use an earth clamp (1) to make connections to pipework. Clean the pipe locally with wire wool to make a good connection between the pipe and clamp, and scrape or strip an area of paintwork if the pipe has been painted.

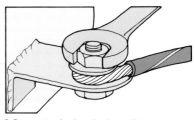

1 Fit an earth clamp to pipework

Connecting to a bath or basin

Metal baths or basins are made with an earth tag. Connect the earth cable by trapping the bared end of the conductor under a nut and bolt with metal washers (2). Make sure the tag has not been painted or enamelled.

If an old bath or basin has not been provided with an earth tag, drill a hole through the foot of the bath or to the rim at the back of the basin and connect the cable with a similar nut and bolt.

2 Connect to bath or basin earth tag

Connecting to an appliance

Connect the earth to the terminal provided in an electrical appliance (3) and run it to a clamp on a metal supply pipe nearby.

3 Fix to an appliance earth terminal

WIRING A SHOWER UNIT

An electrically heated shower unit is plumbed into the mains water supply (▷). The water pressure operates a switch to energize a heater that heats the water on its way to the shower head. Because there is so little time to heat the flowing water instantaneous showers use a heavy load, from 6 to 8kW. Consequently a shower needs a separate radial circuit.

The circuit cable must be 6mm² two-core and earth, protected by a 30amp fuse in a spare fuseway at the consumer unit or in a separate 30amp switchfuse unit. The cable runs directly to the shower unit where it must be wired according to the manufacturer's instructions.

The shower has its own on/off switch but there must also be a separate isolating switch in the circuit. This must not be accessible to anyone using the shower, so install a ceiling-mounted 30amp double-pole pull-cord switch with a contact gap of at least 3mm, and preferably one with a neon 'on' indicator. Fix the backplate of the switch to the ceiling and, having sleeved the earth conductors, connect them to the E terminal on the switch. Connect the conductors from the consumer unit to the 'Mains' terminal of the switch and those of the cable to the shower to the 'Load' terminals (1).

Shower unit, metallic pipes and fittings must be bonded to earth (▷).

Shower circuit
1 Shower
2 30amp ceiling switch
3 Radial circuit
4 Consumer unit

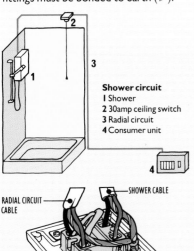

RADIAL CIRCUIT CABLE

SHOWER CABLE

1 **Wiring a 30amp ceiling switch**

BATHROOM HEATERS

Skirting heaters, wall-mounted heaters and oil-filled radiators should be wired to a fused connection unit mounted nearby, between 150mm (6in) and 300mm (1ft) from the floor. Whether the connection to the unit is by flex or cable will depend on the type of heater. Follow the manufacturer's instructions, and fit a 13amp cartridge fuse in the connection unit.

In a bathroom a fused connection unit must be mounted out of reach, so any heater mounted near the floor of a bathroom must be on a cable to a connection unit installed outside the room. If the appliance is fitted with flex, mount a flexible cord outlet (1) next to the appliance, run a cable from the outlet to the fused connection unit outside and connect it to the 'Load' terminals in the unit.

The flex outlet is mounted on a standard surface-mounted pattress or flush on a metal box. At the back of the faceplate are three pairs of terminals to take the conductors from the flex and the cable (2).

Radiant wall heaters for use in bathrooms must be fixed high on the wall and out of reach from shower or bath. A fused connection unit, fitted with a 13amp fuse, must be mounted at the same level and the heater must be controlled by a pull-cord double-pole switch – the type that works by breaking both live and neutral contacts. Many heaters have built-in double-pole switches; otherwise you must fit a ceiling-mounted 15amp double-pole switch between the connection unit and the heater. The switch terminals marked 'Mains' are for the cable on the circuit side of the switch; those marked 'Load' are for the heater side. The earth wires are connected to a common terminal on the switch pattress.

If it is not possible to run a spur to the fused connection unit from a socket outside the bathroom don't be tempted to connect a radiant wall heater to the lighting circuit. Instead run a separate radial circuit from the fused connection to a 5amp fuseway in the consumer unit, using 2.5mm² cable.

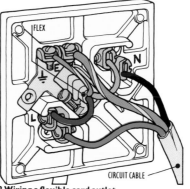

2 **Wiring a flexible cord outlet**

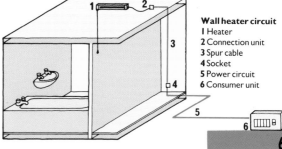

Wall heater circuit
1 Heater
2 Connection unit
3 Spur cable
4 Socket
5 Power circuit
6 Consumer unit

SHAVER SOCKETS

Special shaver outlets are the only sockets allowed in bathrooms. They contain transformers which isolate the user side of the units from the mains, so they cannot cause an electric shock.

A shaver unit can be wired to a spur from a ring circuit or to a junction box on an earthed lighting circuit. Connect the conductors to the shaver unit: red to L, black to N and earth to E (1).

This type of socket conforms to the exacting British Standard, BS 3535, but there are shaver socket outlets which do not have isolating transformers. These are quite safe to install and use in a bedroom but must not be fitted in a bathroom. Wire such an outlet from the lighting circuit or from a fused connection unit on a ring circuit spur. Fit a 3amp fuse.

Shaver unit for use in a bathroom

SEE ALSO

Details for: ▷
Plumbing a shower	40
Bathroom safety	68

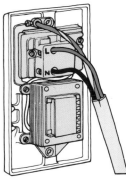

1 **Wiring a shaver unit**

1 **Flexible cord outlet**

FUSED CONNECTION UNITS

IMMERSION HEATERS

A fused connection unit is basically a device for joining circuit wiring to the flex – or sometimes cable – of an appliance. The junction incorporates the added protection of a cartridge fuse like that found in a 13amp plug. If the appliance is connected by a flex, choose a unit with a cord outlet in the faceplate.

Some fused connection units are also switched, with or without a neon indicator that shows when the switch is on. The switched connection unit allows you completely to isolate the appliance from the mains.

All fused connection units are single – there are no double ones – with square faceplates that fit the standard plastic surface-mounted pattresses or the metal boxes for flush mounting.

Fused connection units
1 Unswitched connection unit
2 Switched unit with cord outlet and indicator
3 Connection unit and socket in a dual box

Changing a fuse
With the power off, remove the retaining screw in the face of the fuse holder. Take the holder from the unit, prise out the old fuse and fit a new one. Replace the fuse holder.

Wiring a fused connection unit

Fused connection units can be supplied by a ring circuit, a radial circuit or a spur.

Some appliances are connected to the unit by a length of flex while others are wired up with cable but the wiring arrangements inside the units are the same. Units with cord outlets have clamps to secure the connecting flex.

An unswitched connection unit has two live (L) terminals, one marked 'Load' for the brown wire of the flex, and the other marked 'Mains' for the red wire from the circuit cable. The blue wire from the flex and the black wire from the circuit cable go to similar neutral (N) terminals and both earth wires are connected to the E terminal or terminals (1).

A switched connection unit
A fused connection unit with a switch has two sets of terminals. Those marked 'Mains' are for the spur or ring cable that supplies the power; the terminals marked 'Load' are for the flex or cable from the appliance.

Wire up the flex side first, connecting the brown wire to the L terminal and the blue one to the N terminal, both on the Load side. Connect the green/yellow wire to the E terminal (2) and tighten the cord clamp.

Attach the circuit conductors to the Mains terminals – red to L and black to N, then sleeve the earth wire and take it to the E terminal (2).

If the fused connection unit is on a

ring circuit you must fit two circuit conductors into each Mains terminal and the earth terminal.

Before securing the unit in its box with the fixing screws make sure the wires are held firmly in the terminals and that they can fold away neatly.

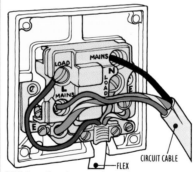

1 Wiring a fused connection unit

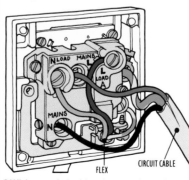

2 Wiring a switched fused connection unit

Water in a storage cylinder is heated by an electric immersion heater, providing a central supply of hot water for the whole house. The heating element, rather like a larger version of the one that heats an electric kettle, is normally sheathed in copper, but more expensive sheathings of incoloy or titanium will increase the life of an element in hard water areas.

Adjusting the water temperature
A thermostat to control the maximum temperature of the water is set by adjusting a screw inside the plastic cap that covers the terminal box (1).

Types of immersion heater
An immersion heater can be installed from the top of the cylinder or from the side, and top-entry units can have single or double elements. In the single-element top-entry type of heater the element extends down almost to the bottom of the cylinder, so that the whole of its contents is heated whenever the heater is switched on (2). For economy one element in the double-element type is a short one that heats only the top half of the cylinder while the other element is a full-length one that is switched on when greater quantities of hot water are needed (3).

A double-element heater with a single thermostat is called a twin-element heater. One with a thermostat for each element is known as a dual-element heater.

Side-entry heaters are the same length, one being positioned near the bottom of the cylinder and the other a little above half way (4). This is a more efficient arrangement for heating water and controlling its temperature.

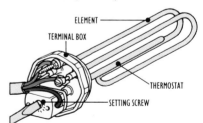

ELEMENT
TERMINAL BOX
THERMOSTAT
SETTING SCREW

1 Adjusting the thermostat

2 Single element   **3 Double element**   **4 Side-entry elements**

HEATING WATER ON THE NIGHT RATE

If you agree to have a special meter installed the Electricity Board will supply you with power at a cheap rate for seven hours between midnight and 8.00 a.m., the hours varying with the time of year.

The scheme is called Economy 7 (▷). Providing you have a cylinder of big enough capacity to store hot water for a day's requirements you can benefit by producing all your hot water during the Economy 7 hours. Even if you heat your water electrically only in the summer it can be worth considering the scheme. For the water to retain its heat all day you must have an efficient insulating jacket fitted to the cylinder or a cylinder already factory-insulated with a layer of heat-retaining foam (▷).

If your cylinder is already fitted with an immersion heater you can use its wiring by fitting an Economy 7 programmer, a device which will switch your immersion heater on automatically at night and heat up the whole cylinder. If you should occasionally run out of hot water during the day you can adjust the programmer's controls to boost the temperature briefly on the more expensive daytime rate.

You can make even greater savings if you have two side-entry immersion heaters or a dual-element one. The programmer will switch on the longer element – or the bottom one – at night, but should you need daytime water-heating only the upper element is used.

You can have a similar arrangement without a programmer by wiring two separate circuits for the elements. The upper element is wired to the daytime supply and the lower one is wired to its own switchfuse unit and operated by the Electricity Board's Economy 7 timeswitch during the hours of the night-time tariff only. A setting of 75°C (167°F) is recommended for the lower element and 60°C (140°F) for the upper one. If you live in a soft water area or have heater elements sheathed in incoloy or titanium you can raise the temperatures to 80°C (175°F) and 65°C (150°F) respectively without reducing lives of the elements.

To ensure that you never run short of hot water leave the upper unit switched on permanently. It will start heating up only when the thermostat detects a temperature of 60°C (140°F), which should happen only rarely if you have a large and properly insulated cylinder.

WIRING THE IMMERSION HEATER

The circuit

Most immersion heaters are rated at 3kW, but while you can usually wire a 3kW appliance to a ring circuit an immersion heater is seen as taking a continuous 3kW, even though rarely switched on continuously. A continuous 3kW load would seriously reduce a ring circuit's capacity, so immersion heaters must have their own radial circuits.

The circuit is run in 2.5mm² two-core and earth cable protected by a 15amp fuse, though a 20amp fuse can be fitted quite safely. Each element must have a two-pole isolating switch mounted near the cylinder, probably marked 'water heater' and having a neon indicator (1). From a flex outlet at the switch a 2.5mm² heat-resistant flex runs to the immersion heater.

If the cylinder is in a bathroom the switch must be inaccessible to anyone using the bath or shower. If this precludes a normal water-heater switch use a 20amp ceiling-mounted pull-switch with a mechanical ON/OFF indicator.

Wiring two side-entry heaters

For simplicity use two switches, one for each heater and marked accordingly.

Wiring the switches
Fix the mounting boxes to the wall, feed a circuit cable to each and wire them in the same way. Strip and prepare the wires, connect them to the 'Mains' terminals – red to L, black to N – sleeve the earth wire and fix it to the common earth terminal (2). Prepare a heat-resistant flex for each switch. At each take the green/yellow earth wire to the common earth terminal, the other wires to the 'Load' terminals – brown to L and blue to N (2) – tighten the flex clamps and screw on the faceplates.

Wiring the heaters
The flex from the upper switch goes to the top heater and that from the lower switch to the bottom one. At each one feed the flex through the hole in the cap and prepare the wires. Connect the brown wire to one terminal on the thermostat (the other terminal on the thermostat is already connected to the wire running to the L terminal of the heating element). Connect the blue wire to the N terminal and green/yellow wire to the E terminal (3) and replace the caps on the terminal boxes.

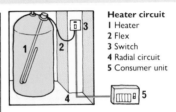

Heater circuit
1 Heater
2 Flex
3 Switch
4 Radial circuit
5 Consumer unit

CIRCUIT CABLE

FLEX TO HEATER

2 Wiring the switch

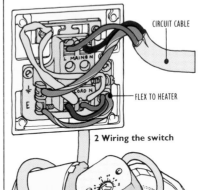

3 Wiring the heater

Running the cable
Run the circuit cables from the cylinder cupboard to the fuseboard and, with the power off, connect the cable from the upper heater to a spare fuseway in the consumer unit. Though the consumer unit is switched off the cable between main switch and meter is live, so take care. Wire the other cable to its own switchfuse unit – or storage-radiator consumer unit if you have one – ready for connecting to the Economy 7 timeswitch.

WIRING A DUAL-ELEMENT HEATER

Wire the circuit as described above but feed the flex from both switches into the cap on the terminal box of the heater. Strip and prepare the wires and connect both blue ones to the same N terminal and both earth wires to the E terminal. Connect the brown wire from the upper switch to the L1 terminal of the elements and the other brown wire to the L2 terminal (4).

SEE ALSO

Details for: ▷	
Insulation	65
Economy 7	77
Switching off electricity	66

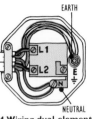

1 20amp switch for immersion heater

EARTH

L1
L2
E
N

NEUTRAL

4 Wiring dual-element

• **Essential tools**
  Sink plunger
  Scriber
  Centre punch
  Steel rule
  Try square
  General-purpose
  hacksaw

PLUMBER'S AND METALWORKER'S TOOL KIT

The growing use of plastics in plumbing is likely to affect the trade considerably, and while plastics have been used for drainage for some years the advent of plastics suitable for mains pressure and hot water will have the greatest impact. But brass fittings and pipework of copper and other metals are still the most commonly used for domestic plumbing, so the plumber's tool kit is still basically a metalworker's one.

SINK AND DRAIN CLEANING EQUIPMENT

There's no need to hire a plumber to clear blocked appliances, pipes or even main drains. The necessary equipment can be bought or hired.

Sink plunger

WC plunger

Plunger
This is a simple but effective tool for clearing a blockage from the trap or WC pan. A pumping action on the rubber cap forces air and water along the pipe to disperse the blockage.

When you buy a plunger make sure that the cup is big enough to surround the waste outlet completely. The cup of a WC plunger may have a cone that makes a tight fit in the trap.

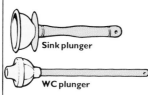

Compressed-air gun
A blocked wastepipe can be cleared with a compressed-air gun. A hand-operated pump compresses air in the gun's reservoir, to be released into the pipe by a trigger. The gun has three interchangeable nozzles to suit different outlets.

WC auger
The short coiled-wire WC auger, designed for clearing WC and gully traps, is rotated by a handle in a hollow rigid shaft. A vinyl guard prevents scratching of the WC pan.

Drain auger

WC auger

Drain auger
A flexible drain auger of coiled wire will pass through small-diameter wastepipes to clear blockages. Pass the corkscrew-like head into the pipe until it reaches the blockage, clamp on the cranked handle and turn it to rotate the head and engage the blockage. Push and pull the auger until the pipe is clear.

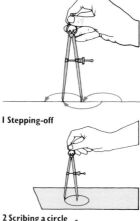

RODS

PLUNGER   CORKSCREW   SCRAPER

Drain rods
You can hire a complete set of rods and fittings for clearing main drains and inspection chambers. Traditionally the rods are of flexible cane and wire, but modern ones come in 1m (3ft 3in) lengths of polypropylene with threaded brass connectors. The clearing heads comprise a double-worm corkscrew fitting, a 100mm (4in) rubber plunger and a hinged scraper for clearing the open channels in inspection chambers.

MEASURING AND MARKING TOOLS

Tools for measuring and marking metal are very like those used for wood but are made and calibrated for greater accuracy because metal parts must fit with great precision.

Scriber
For precise work, mark lines and hole centres on metal with a pointed hardened-steel scriber—but use a pencil to mark the centre of a bend, as a scored line made with a scriber may open up when the metal is stretched on the outside of the bend.

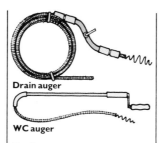

Spring dividers
Spring dividers are like a pencil compass, but both legs have steel points. These are adjusted to the required spacing by a knurled nut on a threaded rod that links the legs.

Using spring dividers
Use dividers to step-off divisions along a line (**1**) or to scribe circles (**2**) . By running one point against the edge of a workpiece you can also scribe a line parallel with the edge (**3**).

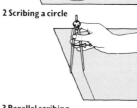

1 Stepping-off

2 Scribing a circle

3 Parallel scribing

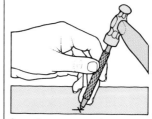

Centre punch
A centre punch is for marking the centres of holes to be drilled.

Correcting a centre mark

Using a centre punch
Place the punch's point on dead centre and strike it with a hammer. If the mark is not accurate, angle the punch toward the true centre, tap it to extend the mark in that direction, then mark the centre again.

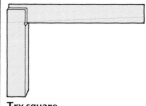

Steel rule
You'll need a long tape measure (◁) for estimating pipe runs and positioning appliances, but use a 300 or 600mm (1 or 2ft) steel rule for marking out components when absolute accuracy is important.

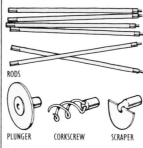

Try square
You can use a woodworker's try square (◁) to mark out or check right angles, but an all-metal engineer's try square is precision-made for metalwork. The small notch between blade and stock allows the tool to fit properly against a right-angled workpiece even when the corner is burred by filing. For general-purpose work, choose a 150mm (6in) try square.

METAL-CUTTING TOOLS

You can cut solid bar, sheet and tubular metal with a hacksaw, but special tools for cutting sheet metal and pipes will give you more accuracy and speed the work.

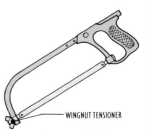

WINGNUT TENSIONER

General-purpose hacksaw
A modern hacksaw has a tubular steel frame with a light cast-metal handle. The frame is adjustable to blades of different lengths, which are tensioned by tightening a wingnut.

CUTTING ASBESTOS

To cut asbestos, wet it to damp-down the dust and wear a face mask. Place plastic sheet under the work to catch falling dust. Carefully fold the sheet and pick up any spilt dust with a damp sponge. Seal it in a plastic bag. Ask your local authority about disposal.

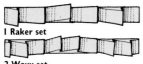

1 Raker set

2 Wavy set

Size and set of teeth
There are fine and coarse hacksaw blades, graded by the number of teeth per 25mm (1in). A coarse blade has 14 to 18 teeth per 25mm (1in) and a fine one has 24 to 32. The teeth are set–bent sideways–to make a cut wider than the blade's thickness and prevent it jamming in the work. Coarse teeth are 'raker set' (**1**), with pairs of teeth bent in opposite directions and every third or fifth one left in line with the blade to clear the cut of metal waste. Fine teeth are too small to be raker set and the whole row is 'wavy set' (**2**).

Use a coarse blade for cutting soft metals like brass and aluminium, which would clog fine teeth, and a fine blade for thin sheet and the harder metals.

Hardness
A hacksaw blade must be harder than the metal it is cutting or its teeth will quickly blunt. A flexible blade with hardened teeth will cut most metals, but there are fully hardened blades that stay sharp longer and are less prone to losing teeth. Being rigid and brittle they break easily. High-speed steel blades for sawing very hard alloys are expensive and even more brittle than the fully hardened ones.

Fitting a hacksaw blade
Adjust the length of the saw frame and slip the blade onto the pins at its end, the teeth pointing away from the handle, then apply tension with the wingnut. If the new blade wanders off line when you work, tighten the wingnut.

If you have to fit a new blade after starting to cut a piece of metal it may jam in the cut because its set is wider than that of the old worn blade. Start a fresh cut on the other side of the workpiece and work back to the cut you began with.

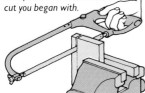

Turning a blade
Sometimes it's easier to work with the blade at right angles to the frame. Rotate the square-section spigots a quarter turn before fitting the blade on the pins.

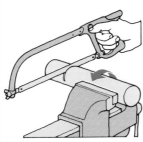

1 Turn first kerf away from you

Sawing metal bar
*Hold the work in an engineer's vice, the marked cutting line as close to the jaws as possible. Start the cut on the waste side of the line with short strokes until it is about 1mm (1/16in) deep, then turn the bar 90 degrees in the vice, so that the cut faces away from you, and make a similar one in the new face (**1**). Continue in this way until the kerf (cut) runs right round the bar, then cut through the remainder with long steady strokes. Steady the end of the saw with your free hand and put a little light oil on the blade if necessary.*

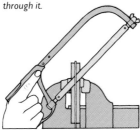

Sawing rod or pipe
As you cut a cylindrical rod or tube with a hacksaw rotate the work away from you until the kerf (cut) goes right round it, then cut through it.

Sawing sheet metal
To saw a small piece of sheet metal, sandwich it between two strips of wood clamped in a vice. Adjust the metal to place the cutting line close to the strips, then saw down the waste side with steady strokes and the blade angled to the work.

Clamp thin sheet metal between two pieces of plywood and cut through all three layers at once.

Sawing a groove
To cut a slot or groove wider than a standard hacksaw blade fit two or more identical blades in the frame at the same time.

Junior hacksaw
Use a junior hacksaw for cutting small-bore tubing and thin metal rod. In most types the blade is held under tension by the spring steel frame.

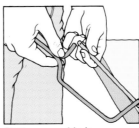

Fitting a new blade
To fit a blade, locate it in the slot at the front of the frame, then bow the frame against a workbench until the blade fits in the rear slot.

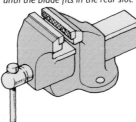

Engineer's vice
A large engineer's or metalworker's vice is bolted to the workbench, but small clamp-on ones are also available. Slip soft fibre liners over the jaws of a vice to protect workpieces held in it.

Cold chisel
Though plumbers use cold chisels to hack old pipework out of masonry they are also for cutting metal rod and slicing the heads off rivets. Keep the tip of yours sharpened on a bench grinder.

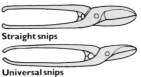

Straight snips

Universal snips

Tinsnips
Tinsnips are heavy-duty scissors for cutting sheet metal. Straight snips have wide blades for cutting straight edges, and if you try to cut curves with them the waste gets caught against the blades, though it's possible to cut a convex curve by removing small straight pieces of waste and working down to the marked line. Universal snips have thick narrow blades that will cut a curve in one pass and will also make straight cuts.

Using tinsnips
As you cut along the marked line let the waste curl away below the sheet. If the metal is too thick to be cut with one hand clamp one handle of the snips in a vice so that you can put your full weight on the other.

Try not to close the jaws completely each time, as it can cause a jagged edge on the metal. Wear thick work gloves when you are cutting sheet metal.

SHARPENING SNIPS

Clamp one handle in a vice and sharpen the edge with a smooth file; repeat with the other and finish by removing the burrs from the backs of the blades on an oiled slipstone.

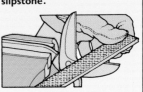

Sheet-metal cutter
Unlike tinsnips, which will distort a narrow waste strip on one side of the cutting line, a sheet-metal cutter removes a narrow strip as perfectly flat as the larger sheet. It is also suited to cutting rigid plastic sheet, which can crack if it is distorted by tinsnips.

Tube cutter
A tube cutter will cut the ends of pipes at exactly 90 degrees to their length. The pipe is clamped between the cutting wheel and an adjustable slide with two rollers, and is cut as the tool is revolved round it and the adjusting screw tightened before each turn. Keep the cutter lightly oiled when you use it.

Chain-link cutter
Cut large-diameter pipes with a chain-link cutter. Wrap the chain round the pipe, locate the end link in the clamp and tighten the adjuster until the cutter on each link bites into the metal. Work the handle back and forth to score the pipe and continue, tightening the adjuster intermittently to cut deeper, until the pipe is severed.

SEE ALSO

Details for: ▷

| Cutting pipe | 21, 29 |

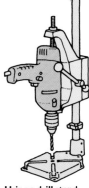

Using a drill stand
To bore holes absolutely square to the face of the work, mount your electric drill in a vertical drill stand.

Sheet-metal cutter

Tube cutter

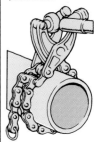

Chain-link cutter

● **Essential tools**
Junior hacksaw
Cold chisel
Tinsnips
Pipe cutter

- **Essential tools**
  High-speed twist drills
  Variable or two-speed
  power drill
  Bending spring
  Soft mallet
  Soldering iron
  Gas torch

DRILLS AND PUNCHES

Special-quality steel bits are made for drilling holes in metal. Cut 12 to 25mm (1/2 to 1 in) holes in sheet metal with a punch.

Twist drills
Metal-cutting twist drills are very like those used for wood but are made from high-speed steel and with tips ground to a shallower angle. Use them in a power drill at slow speeds.

Mark the hole's centre with a centre punch (◁) to locate the drill point and clamp the work in a vice or to the bed of a drill stand (◁). Drill slowly and steadily and keep the bit oiled.

To drill a large hole make a pilot hole first with a small drill to guide the larger one.

When drilling sheet metal the bit may jam and produce a ragged hole as it exits on the far side of the work. To prevent this, clamp the work between pieces of plywood and drill through the three layers.

Hole punch
Use a hole punch to make large holes in sheet metal. Mark the circumference of the hole with spring dividers (◁), lay the metal on a piece of scrap softwood or plywood, place the punch's tip over the marked circle, tap it with a hammer, then check the alignment of the punched ring with the scribed circle. Reposition the punch and, with one sharp hammer blow, cut through the metal. If the wood gives and the metal is slightly distorted, tap it flat again with the hammer.

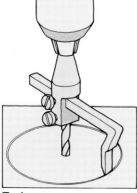

Tank cutter
Use a tank cutter to make holes for pipework in plastic or metal storage cisterns.

METAL BENDERS

Thick or hard metal must be heated before it can be bent successfully, but soft copper piping and sheet metal can be bent while cold.

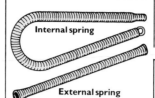

Internal spring

External spring

Bending springs
You can bend small-diameter pipes over your knee, but their walls must be supported with a coiled spring to prevent them buckling.

Push an internal-type spring inside the pipe or an external-type one over it. Either type of spring must fit the pipe exactly.

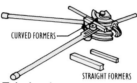

CURVED FORMERS

STRAIGHT FORMERS

Tube bender
In a tube bender, pipe is bent over one of two fixed curved formers that give the optimum radii for plumbing. Each has a matching straight former which is placed between the pipe and a steel roller on a movable lever. When this lever is moved towards the fixed one the pipe is bent over the curved former. The formers support the pipe walls during bending.

You can get extra leverage by clamping the fixed lever in a vice and using both hands on the movable one.

Soft mallet
Soft mallets have heads of coiled rawhide, hard rubber or plastic. They are used in bending strip or sheet metal, which would be damaged by a metal hammer.

To bend sheet metal at a right angle, clamp it between stout battens along the bending line. Start at one end and bend the metal over one of the battens by tapping it with the mallet. Don't attempt the full bend at once but work along the sheet, increasing the angle and keeping it constant along the length until the metal lies flat on the batten, then knock out any kinks.

TOOLS FOR JOINING METAL

You can make permanent watertight joints between metal components by using a molten alloy that acts like a glue when it cools and solidifies. Mechanical fixings like compression joints, rivets and nuts and bolts are also used for joining metal.

SOLDERS
Solders are special alloys for joining metals and are designed to melt at temperatures lower than the melting points of the metals to be joined. Soft solder, a tin-and-lead alloy, melts at 183 to 250°C. Brazing, a method of hard soldering involving a copper and zinc alloy, requires the even higher temperature of some 850 to 1000°C.

Solder is available as a coiled wire or a thick rod. Use soft solder for copper plumbing fittings.

FLUX
To be soldered, a joint must be perfectly clean and free of oxides. Even after cleaning with wire wool or emery, oxides will form immediately, preventing a positive bond between solder and metal. Flux forms a chemical barrier against oxidation. Corrosive, or 'active' flux, applied with a brush, actually dissolves oxides but must be washed from the surface with water as soon as the solder solidifies or it will go on corroding the metal. A 'passive' flux, in paste form, is used where it will be impossible to wash the work thoroughly. Though a passive flux will not dissolve oxide it will exclude it adequately for soldering copper plumbing joints and electrical connections.

Some wire solder contains flux in its hollow core. The flux flows fractionally before the solder melts.

Soldering irons
Successful soldering needs the work to be made hot enough to melt the solder and cause it to flow; otherwise the solder will solidify before it can completely penetrate the joint. The necessary heat is applied with a soldering iron.

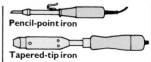
Pencil-point iron

Tapered-tip iron

There are simple irons that are heated in a fire, but an electric iron is much handier to use and its temperature is both controllable and constant. Use a low-powered pencil-point iron for soldering electrical connections and a larger one with a tapered tip to bring sheet metal up to working temperature.

Tinning a soldering iron
The tip of a soldering iron must be coated with solder to keep it oxide-free and maintain its performance. Clean the cool tip with a file, then heat it to working temperature, dip it in flux and apply a stick of solder to coat it evenly.

Using a soldering iron
Clean the mating surfaces of the joint to a bright finish and coat them with flux, then clamp the joint tightly between two wooden battens. Apply the hot iron along the joint to heat the metal thoroughly, then run its tip along the edge of the joint, following it with solder. Solder will flow immediately into a properly heated joint.

Gas torch
Even a large soldering iron cannot heat thick metal fast enough to compensate for heat loss away from the joint, and this is very much the situation when you solder pipework (◁). Though the copper unions have very thin walls the pipe on each side dissipates so much heat that an iron cannot get the joint itself hot enough to form a watertight soldered seal. Use a gas torch with an intensely hot flame that will heat the work quickly.

The torch runs on liquid gas contained under pressure in a disposable metal canister that screws onto the gas inlet. Open the control valve and light the gas released from the nozzle, then adjust the valve until the flame roars and is bright blue. Use the hottest part of the flame–about the middle of its length–to heat the joint.

Fibreglass mat
Buy a fireproof mat of fibreglass from a plumbers' merchant to protect flammable surfaces from the heat of a gas torch.

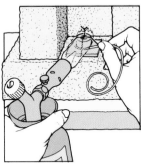

Hard-soldering and brazing
Use a gas torch to hard-solder or braze. Clean and flux the work – if possible with an active flux – then wire or clamp the parts together. Place the assembly on a fireproof mat or surround it with firebricks. Bring the joint to red heat with the torch, then dip a stick of the appropriate alloy in flux and apply it to the joint. When the joint is cool chip off hardened flux, wash the metal thoroughly in hot water and finish the joint with a file.

Hot air gun
Some hot air guns, designed for stripping old paintwork, can also be used for soft soldering. You can vary the temperature of an electronic gun from 100 to 600° C. A heat shield on the nozzle reflects the heat back onto the work.

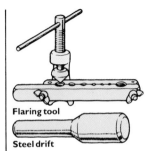

Flaring tool

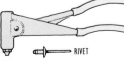

Steel drift

Flaring tools
To make a non-manipulative joint (▷) in plumbing pipework the ends of the copper pipes are simply cut square and cleaned up to remove sharp edges. For a manipulative joint (▷) the pipe ends must be flared to lock into the joint.

The simplest way to flare a copper pipe is with a steel drift. First slip one joint cap-nut onto the pipe, then push the narrow shank of the drift into the pipe. Strike the tool with a heavy hammer to drive its conical part into the pipe, stretching the walls to the required shape.

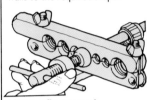

Using a flaring tool
A proper flaring tool will shape pipework more accurately. Again with the cap-nut in place, clamp the pipe in the matching hole in the die block, its end flush with the side of the block, then turn the screw of the flaring tool to drive its cone into the pipe.

━━━━━ RIVET

Blind riveter
Join thin sheet metal with a blind riveter, a hand-operated tool with plier-like handles. The special rivets have long shanks that break off and leave slightly raised heads on both sides of the work.

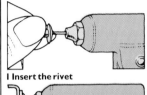

I Insert the rivet

2 Squeeze the handles

Using a riveter
Clamp the two sheets together and drill holes right through the metal, matching the diameter of the rivets and spaced regularly along the joint. Open the handles of the riveter and insert the rivet shank in the head (1). Push the rivet through a hole in the work and, while pressing the tool hard against the metal, squeeze the handles to compress the rivet head on the far side (2). When the rivet is fully expanded the shank will snap off in the tool.

SPANNERS AND WRENCHES

A plumber uses a great variety of spanners and wrenches on a wide range of fittings and fixings, but you can hire the ones that you need only occasionally.

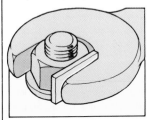

Open-ended spanner
A set of the familiar open-ended spanners is essential to a plumber or metalworker. In most situations pipework runs into a fitting or accessory and it is not possible to use anything but a spanner with open jaws. Most spanners are double-ended, perhaps in a combination of metric and imperial sizes, and sizes are duplicated within a set for when two identical nuts have to be manipulated simultaneously, as on a compression joint, for instance.

Achieving a tight fit
A spanner must be a good fit or it will round over the corners of the nut. You can pack out the jaws with a thin 'shim' of metal if a snug fit is otherwise not possible.

Ring spanner
Being a closed circle, the head of a ring spanner is stronger and fits better than that of an open-ended one. It is specially handy for loosening corroded nuts if it can be slipped onto them from above.

Square nut   **Hexagonal nut**

Choosing a ring spanner
Choose a 12-point spanner. It is fast to use and will fit both square and hexagonal nuts. You can buy combination spanners with rings at one end and open jaws at the other.

Box spanner
A box spanner is a steel tube with its ends shaped into hexagons – an excellent tool for reaching a nut in a confined space. Turning force is applied with a tommy bar slipped into a hole drilled through the spanner. Don't use a very long bar. Too much leverage may strip the thread of the fitting or distort the thin walls of the spanner.

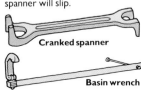

Adjustable spanner
Having a movable jaw, an adjustable spanner is not as strong as an open-ended or ring spanner but is often the only tool that will fit a large or over-painted nut. Make sure the spanner fits the nut snugly by rocking it slightly as you tighten the jaws. Grip the nut with the roots of the jaws. If you use just the tips they can spring apart slightly under force and the spanner will slip.

Cranked spanner

Basin wrench

Cranked spanner and basin wrench
A cranked spanner is a special double-ended wrench for use on tap connectors (▷).

A basin wrench, for the same job, has a pivoting jaw that can be set for either tightening or loosening a fitting.

Radiator spanner
Use a simple spanner of hexagonal-section steel rod to remove radiator blanking plugs (▷). One end is ground to fit plugs with square sockets.

● **Essential tools**
Blind riveter
Set of open-ended spanners
Small and large adjustable spanners

SEE ALSO

◁ Details for:
Disconnecting pipes   22

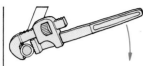

Stilson wrench

The adjustable toothed jaws of a stilson wrench are for gripping pipework. As force is applied the jaws tighten on the work.

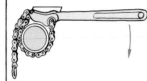

Chain wrench

A chain wrench does the same job as a stilson wrench but it can be used on very large-diameter pipes and fittings. Wrap the chain tightly round the work and engage it with the hook at the end of the wrench, then lever the handle towards the toothed jaw to apply turning force.

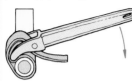

Strap wrench

With a strap wrench you can disconnect chromed pipework without damaging its surface. Wrap the smooth leather or canvas strap round the pipe, pass its end through the slot in the head of the tool and pull it tight. Leverage on the handle will rotate the pipe.

Plier wrench

A plier wrench locks onto the work. It will grip round stock or damaged nuts and is often used as a small cramp.

Using a plier wrench

Squeeze the handles to close the jaws while slowly turning the adjusting screw clockwise until they snap together (1). Release the tool's grip on the work by pulling the release lever (2).

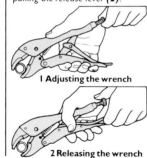

I Adjusting the wrench

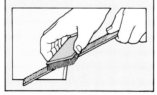

2 Releasing the wrench

● **Essential tools**
Plier wrench
Second-cut and smooth flat files
Second-cut and smooth half-round files

FILES

Files are used for shaping and smoothing metal components and removing sharp edges.

CLASSIFYING FILES

The working faces of a file are composed of parallel ridges, or teeth, set at about 70 degrees to its edges. A file is classified according to the size and spacing of its teeth and whether it has one or two sets.

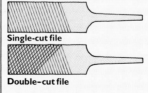

Single-cut file

Double-cut file

A **single-cut file** has one set of teeth virtually covering each face. A **double-cut file** has a second set of identical teeth crossing the first at a 45-degree angle. Some files are single-cut on one side and double-cut on the other.

The spacing of the teeth relates directly to their size: the finer the teeth the more closely packed they are. Degrees of coarseness are expressed in numbers of teeth per 25mm (1in). Use progressively finer files to shape a component and gradually to remove marks left by coarser ones.

File classification

Bastard file – Coarse grade (26 teeth per 25mm) – For initial shaping. *Second-cut file* – Medium grade (36 teeth per 25mm) – For preliminary smoothing. *Smooth file* – Fine grade (47 teeth per 25mm) – For final smoothing.

CLEANING A FILE

Soft metal clogs the teeth of files but can be removed by brushing along the teeth with a file card—a fine wire brush. Chalk rubbed on a clean file will reduce clogging.

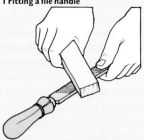

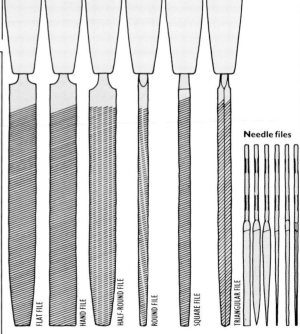

Needle files

FLAT FILE HAND FILE HALF-ROUND FILE ROUND FILE SQUARE FILE TRIANGULAR FILE

Flat file

A flat file tapers from its pointed tang to its tip, both in width and thickness. Both faces and both edges are toothed.

Hand file

Hand files are parallel-sided but tapered in their thickness. Most of them have one smooth edge for filing up to a corner without damaging it.

Half-round file

This tool has one rounded face for shaping inside curves.

Round file

A round file is for shaping tight curves and enlarging holes.

Square file

This file is for cutting narrow slots and smoothing the edges of small rectangular holes.

Triangular file

The triangular file is for accurately shaping and smoothing undercut apertures of less than 90 degrees.

Needle files

Needle files are miniature versions of standard files and are all made in extra-fine grades. They are used for precise work and to sharpen brace bits.

FILE SAFETY

Always fit a wooden or plastic handle on the tang of a file before using it.

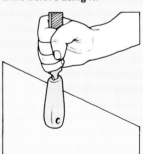

I Fitting a file handle

2 Knock a handle from the tang

If an unprotected file catches on the work, the tang could be driven into the palm of your hand. Having fitted a handle, tap its end on a bench to tighten its grip (1).

To remove a handle, hold the file in one hand and strike the ferrule away from you with a piece of wood (2).

GLOSSARY OF TERMS

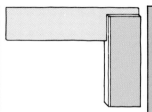

Try square
A try square is used to check the accuracy of square joints and planed timber, also for marking out timber which is to be sawn or cut 'square' to its edge. Look for a try square with its blade and stock (handle) cut from one L-shaped piece of metal. One with a straight blade riveted to the stock may lose its accuracy.

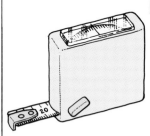

Tape measure and folding rule
A folding boxwood rule is the traditional cabinet-maker's tool for measuring, but a modern retractable steel tape measure is more versatile. Some can take measurements up to about 5m (16ft), including internal ones using the tip of the tape and the back of the case. The tape can be locked open at any point. Avoid letting the spring-loaded tape snap back into its case or the riveted hook on its end will become loose.

Slip-joint or waterpump pliers
The special feature of slip-joint pliers is a movable pivot for enlarging the jaw spacing. The extra-long handles give a good grip on pipes and other fittings.

Radiator roller
A decorator's tool used to paint behind a wall-hung radiator but it is equally useful for applying sheets of insulated foil to the wall behind the radiator in order to reflect heat back into the room.

Airlock
A blockage in a pipe caused by a trapped bubble of air.
Appliance
A machine or device powered by electricity. or A functional piece of equipment connected to the plumbing – a basin, sink, bath etc.

Back-siphonage
The siphoning of part of a plumbing system caused by the failure of mains pressure.
Balanced flue
A ducting system which allows a heating appliance, such as a boiler, to draw fresh air from, and discharge gases to, the outside of a building.
Bore
The hollow part of a pipe or tube.
Burr
The rough raised edge left on a workpiece after cutting or filling.

Cap-nut
The nut used to tighten a fitting onto pipework.
Cesspool
A covered or buried tank for the collection and storage of sewage.
Chase
The groove cut in masonry or plaster to accept pipework or an electrical cable. or To cut such grooves.
Cistern
A water-storage tank such as found in the roof of a house or to service a water closet.
Consumer unit
A box situated near the meter which contains the fuses or MCBs protecting all the circuits. It also houses the main isolating switch which cuts the power to the whole house.

Draincock
A tap from which a plumbing system or appliance is drained.

Economy 7
An Electricity Board scheme which allows you to charge storage heaters and heat water at less than half the general-purpose rate.

Float valve
A water inlet which is closed by the action of a float-operated arm when the water in a cistern reaches the required level.

Gully
The open end of a drainage system at ground level, containing a water-filled trap.

Head
The height of the surface of water above a specific point – used as a measurement of pressure; for example, a head of 2m.
Hopperhead
The funnel-shaped end of a vertical drainage pipe which receives the discharge from other waste pipes.

IEE Regulations
See Wiring Regulations
Insulation – electrical
Nonconductive material surrounding electrical wires or connections to prevent the passage of electricity.
Insulation – thermal
Materials used to reduce the transmission of heat. Insulating a hot-water cylinder and the roof are the most cost-effective measures.
Ladder stay
A device which holds the top of a ladder away from a wall so that one can service overhanging guttering, for instance, without having to lean back and possibly overbalance.

MCB
See Miniature circuit breaker.
Miniature circuit breaker
A special switch installed in a consumer unit to protect an individual circuit. When a fault occurs, the circuit breaker switches off automatically.

Overflow pipe
A drainage pipe designed to discharge safely water which has risen above its intended level in a cistern.

Penetrating damp
Moisture which permeates the fabric of a house due to faulty building techniques or disrepair.
PTFE
Polytetrafluorethylene – used to make tape for sealing threaded plumbing fittings.

Rising main
The pipe which supplies water under mains pressure, usually to a storage cistern in the roof.

Septic tank
A sewage-storage tank, similar to a cesspool, but the waste is treated to render it harmless before it is discharged into a local waterway or underground.
Service pipe
The supply pipe bringing water into a house and which is connected to the rising main.
Shoe
The component forming the lower end of a vertical drainage pipe and which throws water clear of a wall into an open gully.
Spur
A short length of electrical cable feeding a socket outlet or fused connection unit and taking its power from another similar accessory.
Stopcock
A valve which closes a pipe to prevent the passage of water.
Stud partition
An interior timber-framed wall clad with plaster, plasterboard or other sheet material.

Thermostat
A device which maintains a heating system at a constant temperature.
Trap
A bent section of pipe containing standing water to prevent the passage of gases.

Water closet
A lavatory flushed by water.
Water hammer
A vibration in plumbing pipework produced by fluctuating water pressure.
WC
See water closet.
Wiring Regulations
A code of professional practice laid down by the Institution of Electrical Engineers.
Workpiece
An object being shaped, produced or otherwise worked upon. Sometimes shortened to 'work'.

INDEX